WILD HORSE CREEK 2

Coyote Canyon

SHARON SIAMON

Coyote Canyon

Contents

CHAPTER 1
Spanish Horses

"Diego's foal looks exactly like his dad!" Liv Winchester leaned forward in her saddle to watch the blue roan colt race down the dry streambed of Wild Horse Creek. "Look – he's coming to say hello."

Liv and her twin sister Sophie were on their way to the Silver Spur guest ranch. They'd stopped to see the colt – the newest member of a small band of Spanish horses belonging to their grandparents.

Liv rode Cactus Jack, a handsome chestnut with a white blaze, four white socks and a white patch shaped like a cactus on his flank. Sophie's beloved horse, named Cisco, was a glowing sorrel with a lighter mane and tail. The twins had groomed both horses carefully for this trip to the Silver Spur: brushed their flowing manes, curried their smooth hides till they gleamed and polished their small, hard hoofs to show off their proud heritage. Cactus Jack and Cisco were part Arab, part Spanish Barb, and true Spanish colonial horses of the American Southwest.

Diego's colt pranced up to Cisco and licked his lips to show he was a baby needing love and attention. Cisco bowed his head and blew softly. At this, the colt tossed up his head, wheeled around and dashed away – an invitation to Cisco to chase him.

"The colt is adorable, but he'll be in trouble if he runs too far away." Sophie's dark eyes followed the little blue roan anxiously. "Granddad says Diego's herd has been losing foals to the cougars in this canyon." Sophie had been in Arizona only a few weeks but she already knew the desert was full of dangers, from rattlesnakes to hungry cougars.

"Don't worry. Diego will look after him." Liv pointed to where the huge stallion stood guard on a rocky outcrop above the grazing horses. Like his small son, Diego was a striking steel blue, with a long black mane and tail. His band of mares and foals ranged freely in Wild Horse Creek Canyon, where a spring provided water and green grass.

"Is Diego strong enough to protect his herd? Sophie flicked a fly off Cisco's shiny sorrel hide. She couldn't help worrying. Recently Diego had been in a fight with a strange black stallion here on their grandparents' ranch. Nobody knew where the black stallion had come from or where he had gone, but he had left Diego badly hurt.

"Of course he can protect them. Listen! He's calling the colt back." The stallion gave a ringing neigh that echoed from the canyon walls.

The runaway colt did not obey the call. He stopped, turned, planted his feet and looked at his tall, proud father. Then he flicked his fuzzy tail and frisked into a smaller side canyon, out of sight of Diego and the other horses.

Above the canyon floor bed rose steep walls of red rock. Long ago a stream had cut through layers of sandstone, forming ledges and overhangs that were perfect places for hunting cougars to perch and watch for prey.

Sophie and Liv watched the foal dash first in one direction, then another. He pranced up to a flowering bush, spread his spindly front legs and reached down so he could sniff the flowers.

The bush exploded. A hungry gray coyote had been hiding behind it, waiting for the foal to stray near enough to pounce.

It leaped for the foal's throat.

The foal gave a piercing squeal, wheeled around and dashed for safety. Before Liv or Sophie could move, Diego had hurtled from his perch on the rock, thundering to the rescue with an ear-splitting screech of rage.

But the stallion was not as fast as the foal's mother – a swift sorrel mare named Carmelita. Without a sound, the mare raced toward her threatened colt and the coyote close behind.

The coyote snapped at the foal's hamstrings, trying to cripple him. He didn't see Carmelita until the mare was almost on top of him, head down, ears back, jaws wide.

Coyote fur flew in all directions as Carmelita attacked in full fury. The coyote was lucky to escape her trampling hoofs. It fled up the canyon's side, limping.

Meanwhile, the colt scampered back to the main canyon, and Diego came to meet his son. They touched noses. The foal followed meekly behind the stallion as they returned to the herd with Carmelita, still watchful, close by his side.

"Wow!" Liv breathed. "I didn't realize a skinny little coyote would attack a foal. Good thing it wasn't a cougar."

"I hope that experience teaches the colt to stay near his mother," Sophie said with a shudder. "If it hadn't been for Carmelita, Diego's foal would have been that coyote's lunch." She looked up at the jutting rock ledges with their shadowed hiding places. "We should call that place Coyote Canyon from now on."

"And speaking of names, we can't keep calling the little guy Diego's foal," Liv said. "He needs a name of his own."

"A name that suits him – something Spanish," Sophie nodded.

"He waves that tail of his like a flag." Liv pointed to the colt's fuzzy bottlebrush tail. "We could call him *Bandera* – that's Spanish for flag."

"How do you know that?" Sophie stared at her slim, dark-haired sister. They'd only come from Vancouver a few weeks ago to visit their grandparents' Arizona ranch, the Lucky Star. From the beginning, Sophie had felt lost in this vast, empty desert. If it hadn't been for Cisco and a certain young cowboy, she'd have been miserable here. Liv, on the other hand, loved every spiny cactus, thorny bush and dry gully on the Lucky Star. But that was typical of her twin sister, thought Sophie as she brushed a fly off Cisco's neck. Liv always plunged into things head first – like learning Spanish.

Liv turned in her saddle, a slow flush spreading across her high cheekbones. "Temo's been teaching me a few words," she explained.

"So that's it!" Sophie's lips twitched into a smile. Temo was the Mexican-American ranch hand who worked on the guest ranch where they were headed now. Sophie knew Liv was dying to see him again.

"He also said my eyes were *hermosos*," Liv sighed. "That means beautiful in Spanish."

Sophie laughed. "Beautiful eyes, eh? Don't get too stuck on that guy. He's seventeen going on eighteen and you're only thirteen – remember?" But Temo was right about Liv's brown eyes, thought Sophie. They were lovely – wide open and sparkling with life.

"We'll be fourteen in September," Liv reminded her. "And anyway, you're a fine one to talk." She clucked to Cactus Jack and moved off up the canyon trail. "How about you and Shane? You're always gazing up at that tall, skinny cowboy with stars in your eyes. At least I try to hide my feelings about Temo."

"That's different. Shane and I are just friends." Sophie urged Cisco forward, following Liv. She wished Liv wouldn't tease her about Shane. He was the most perfect, most adorable guy Sophie had ever seen. She loved the way his cowboy hat sat low on his head, the way he rode his paint horse Navajo, the way he smiled at her. She wished he – Sophie didn't even know what she wished – except that she was older so Shane would take her seriously.

But even if she were older, why would he notice her with Liv around? They weren't identical twins, not by a long shot. Liv was gorgeous, Sophie thought with a sigh. She was tall with longer legs and wider shoulders than Sophie. Her hair was thicker and shinier. Her smile lit up her face like a hundred-watt lightbulb.

"Don't give me that story." Liv interrupted her thoughts. "I've seen how happy you are that Shane Tripp practically lives at our ranch now that Gran and Granddad are away."

Now it was Sophie's turn to blush. "It's a lucky thing for Mom and for us that he does," she shot back. "Shane's doing all Granddad's work on the ranch, plus his own." Sophie, Liv and their mother had originally come just for spring break but stayed when it turned out Gran's medical treatments in nearby Tucson were going to take months, not days, to complete. Until her grandparents returned to the ranch, Shane would be coming every day to help with chores.

Sophie sped up on Cisco to ride beside Liv. "And he's not doing it because he has a crush on me. He'd do anything to help Gran and Granddad."

She changed the subject as Cisco fell into step beside Cactus Jack. "Gran will want to name Diego's colt herself," she said. "You know how much these horses mean to her."

Liv nodded. "I know. She calls them the soul of the Lucky Star ranch, the last of the horses that came with her great-grandmother Maria Lopez from Mexico. If anything happened to them . . ." Liv shook back her dark hair and straightened her shoulders. "But nothing *is* going to happen to them. So, until she gets back from Tucson, we can call the colt *Bandera*."

"All right." Sophie looked back over her shoulder to where the colt was scampering up and down the creek. "How about Bando for short?"

"Bando it is." Liv surged ahead on Cactus Jack. "Come on, slowpoke. I can't wait to show off Cactus Jack and Cisco and see the inside of the Silver Spur ranch." The two girls had been invited by the owner's sixteen-year-old daughter Dayna Regis to spend a free day at the ranch spa as newcomers to the area.

"I wish we weren't going," Sophie glanced back at the colt again. "I don't feel right leaving Bando out here in the canyon with all these predators around. Maybe the herd should come back to the corral at the ranch until Diego's one hundred percent recovered."

"It was Shane's idea to let them run free." Liv's eyes gleamed with mischief. "Are you doubting him?"

"No, but maybe he'll change his mind when he hears what happened today." Sophie gave her shoulders a firm little shake. "Imagine how he'd feel if we lost Bando." She couldn't get the image of the coyote's jaws snapping at the colt's heels out of her mind.

"Quit worrying and get Cisco moving," Liv urged. "Dayna and her friends will be waiting for us at the Silver Spur."

CHAPTER 2
Horse Style

"Should we ask Dayna Regis and her friends for advice about Bando?" Sophie asked Liv as they tied their horses to the Silver Spur's fancy hitching rail. "They've had experience with coyotes and cougars."

Liv straightened her jeans over the tops of her boots and tucked in her pale blue shirt. "Don't you dare say a word about Granddad's horses to Dayna," she exclaimed. "You know her father would like to get rid of the whole herd."

"Dayna's father scares me." Sophie gave Cisco a final pat. He rested his head on her shoulder as if he knew she hated to leave him there. "What if we run into Mr. Regis?" she asked Liv. Just days ago, he had used the black stallion's appearance as an excuse to round up the Lucky Star horses and try to ship them off.

"What would Sam Regis be doing here at the spa?" Liv shook her head. "I'll bet we won't even catch a glimpse of the old grump today." She threw back her shoulders and took a deep breath. "Ready? Let's go."

She held open a black iron gate decorated with wrought-iron horses. Sophie smoothed down her plaid shirt, pushed her fine brown hair behind her ears and stepped into the garden of the Silver Spur Guest Ranch. It seemed a blissfully cool oasis after the blistering April sun of the Arizona desert. Green leafy trees had been trimmed to form a shady overhead canopy. The low stucco buildings nestled behind screens of flowering shrubs and cacti.

"It's beautiful," Sophie sighed with a note of envy in her voice. "So different from our grandparents' ranch. Dry and Dusty would have been a better name for it than the Lucky Star."

Everywhere in the garden were images of horses. Two rearing stone horses formed a fountain that sat in the center of a pool edged with running horses.

"That must be the entrance to the spa." Liv pointed to a heavy wood plank door with a silver spur as a door knocker.

"I'm nervous." Sophie hung back as Liv reached for the door knocker. "What if Dayna's friends don't like us? We're younger than they are."

"We'll have to meet them sometime." Liv lifted the knocker and banged it down three times. "We might as well get it over with. Anyway, who could not like you? You're smart, pretty and you agree with everything people say."

While the girls waited for the door to open, Liv studied her twin sister. Sophie was much better looking, she thought for the millionth time, with her delicate clear complexion, her small, straight nose and perfectly shaped lips. Sophie's figure was better, too, slender and fine-boned. She had always looked better in the identical clothes their mother had bought them when they were little. And now, when they chose their own wardrobe, it was Sophie who had style. Without even trying, she always looked good.

Sophie still hesitated. "What if Dayna stuffs us in one of her tanning beds? Maybe we should just get back on our horses and leave."

In their brief acquaintance, Dayna had let the girls know that she thought their skin was too pale and had offered them free tanning treatments. But it wasn't only her high and mighty attitude that Liv and Sophie held against her. They'd seen how she treated Temo, as if he were invisible just because he worked for them.

I might see Temo today, Liv thought, her heart beating faster. *He might even come to the door.* She knocked again.

But it was Dayna who threw open the door, looking regal as usual in a two-piece bathing suit, a sleeveless see-through cover-up and flip-flops decorated with horses' heads. She was tanned from head to toe.

"Howdy, gals," she drawled. "Come on in."

Liv and Sophie stepped over the threshold into a large,

low-ceilinged room. Soft music with a western twang played in the background. Painted pots filled with twisted mesquite branches stood on the Mexican tile floor, and brightly striped blankets called *serapes* were draped over cowhide couches.

"Hang your hats here." Dayna motioned to hooks fashioned from spurs on the wall. "The other girls are already soaking in the mineral hot springs. We're lucky – we've got the whole pool to ourselves for an hour."

As they hung their wide-brimmed cowboy hats on the hooks, Sophie grabbed Liv's arm. "We didn't bring bathing suits," she hissed in her sister's ear.

Dayna overheard. "Don't worry about that. We've got a bikini grab bag full of tops and bottoms that will fit you." She started down a wide hall. "C'mon, the pool's this way. You two are gonna just lo-ove it!" She tossed back her blonde pigtails and disappeared through another set of doors.

"I'm not going to love it." Sophie hissed at Dayna's departing back. "What are they doing with swimming pools and fountains at this place? I thought they were short of water. Isn't that why they wanted Granddad's land, and his spring? Isn't that why they wanted to get rid of the horses – so they could claim the land wasn't being used for anything?"

They went through the door, down a flight of stairs and into a changing room with white towels and a basket of bathing suits on a bench.

Liv picked out a skimpy flowered bikini. "Tie this for me." She turned her back to Sophie. "And try not to be so negative. Whatever her father is like, Dayna's doing her best to be nice to us; you can see that."

❊ ❊ ❊ ❊ ❊

"This here is Cheyenne Chase and Hailey Fletcher." Dayna introduced two girls lounging half-submerged against the rocks around the pool. "They're both neighbors of yours so I thought you should get acquainted."

"These are Mr. Starr's granddaughters I told you about," she explained to the girls in the pool. "They come from *up north.*"

"Come on in," the girl named Cheyenne called. "The water feels great."

The small pool was beautiful, Sophie thought, set in a circle of rocks overlooking a sweep of desert outside floor-to-ceiling windows. Far off, the Sierra Madre Mountains poked into the sky. Up close, a herd of beautiful palomino horses, heads down, munched hay in a large corral.

Sophie wished she didn't feel so white and naked in the small bikini. She let Liv jump into the pool ahead of her.

Liv came up gasping and laughing. "You didn't tell me about the whirlpool jets coming at you from all sides!"

"It's not for swimmin'," Hailey called back. Her short

blonde hair was still dry. "It's for relaxation, and we call it the gossip pit 'cause we talk about all our friends and what they're doin'."

I'll bet they've been talking plenty about us, Sophie thought as she hesitated on the pool's edge. *How I got lost in the desert and Liv almost fell off a cliff and how we have to stay and go to school here – maybe for months!*

She and Liv had always lived in a big city on the ocean, crowded and green. Here the earth was brown and dry, and people and animals were scattered like ants on a picnic table. Shane said it took ten acres of this desert to feed one cow!

At the thought of Shane, Sophie summoned her courage and slipped into the pool. Shane thought she was brave, so she'd be brave. The water was warm and smelled funny, and the jets blasted her from every direction, but she made her way over to Liv and the three girls on the other side.

There was a moment of silence while they sized one another up. Hailey was tall and blonde like Dayna, Cheyenne tiny and dark. Both girls looked strong and athletic and had the western look in their eyes that came from a lifetime of staring off into wide spaces.

"Dayna says you know Shane," Cheyenne said. "He's related to me."

"Do you like it at the Lucky Star Ranch?" Hailey asked.

"What do you two say to a ride after our swim?" Dayna looked from Sophie to Liv. "We can have our massage and manicure after lunch."

"Yes!" Liv instantly agreed. "I'd love to see around the ranch."

"Good idea," Sophie joined in. She was glad they wouldn't have to leave Cisco and Cactus Jack any longer than they had to. And riding would give Liv a chance to see Temo, which was what she'd really come for today. It was so easy to tell what Liv was thinking.

CHAPTER 3
Confrontation at the Corral

Liv looked for Temo's black cowboy hat and listened eagerly for the jangle of his spurs as the five girls, showered and dressed in jeans, long-sleeved shirts, western hats and boots, trooped out to the Silver Spur corral.

"Where's Temo?" she blurted to Dayna before she could stop herself.

Dayna gave her a curious glance. "Why do you care? Anybody would think you had a crush on that boy, but of course he's way too old for you." She turned to the corral and pointed. "That's my new horse, that palomino mare with the white snip on her nose. Her name is Champagne."

"She's fabulous." Liv climbed the corral rails to get a better look at the mare. The Silver Spur herd was made up of champion palominos, raised for horse shows and rodeo events. Champagne lifted her head and gave the watching girls a long, considering look, then went back to calmly eating hay.

"How old is she?" Sophie asked, climbing up beside Liv. Cheyenne and Hailey leaned against the fence rails next to Dayna.

"She's seven. I've just started training her on the barrels," she explained. "I think she's going to be great."

"What are the barrels?" Liv hopped off the fence to ask.

The three Arizona girls gaped at her as if she'd asked the dumbest question in the world and then burst out laughing.

"Barrel racing – you know – where we ride the horse around the barrels?" Dayna made circling motions with her hand.

"We've seen it –" Sophie nudged Liv with her elbow. "On TV – in the rodeo."

"Oh, sure." Liv went back to watching Champagne to hide her humiliation.

The next moment was even worse.

Behind them boomed an angry voice. "What are you two girls from the Lucky Star Ranch doing on my spread?"

Liv and Sophie turned to see Dayna's father, Sam Regis, glowering at them. Sam was a short, powerful-looking man, with a large white hat and a red face.

"They are my guests, Daddy," Dayna drawled. "I asked them here."

"And I'm askin' them to leave," Sam Regis growled. "I don't want any relations of old Ted Starr around here."

"Daddy, that's just plain rude." Dayna had her hands on her hips and her head thrown back. "We're goin' for a ride now."

"Not on my horses!"

"No, Daddy, they brought their own horses. And when we come back from our ride we're havin' lunch in the dining room, and they'll be my guests."

"They will not." Sam's face grew purple.

"I checked it with Mama and she said yes." Dayna was not backing down.

If Liv had spoken to her father like that she knew she'd be in a lot of trouble. Dayna clearly didn't respect her Dad or obey him. She and Sam were now nose to nose.

"I don't know why you should take such a dislike to Sophie and Liv just because you don't care for their Granddad," Dayna declared.

Liv knew why. She and Sophie and Shane had been on the Silver Spur ranch the night Sam Regis had tried to steal their grandparents' horses, all the while pretending he was protecting them from the mysterious black stallion. *I wasn't very polite to him*, Liv thought. *I might have even called him names. But that's because he was lying to us.*

She wasn't surprised that Sam didn't want to explain any of this to Dayna. Instead, he turned on the high heels of his cowboy boots and stormed away. "Don't let them touch my horses – do you hear?" he shot over his shoulder.

"I'm sorry." Dayna looked after him. Her face was regaining its normal color. "Daddy can act peculiar sometimes, but don't worry. We just don't pay him any attention, Mama and me, when he's like this." She smiled at Liv and Sophie. "You two go get your horses and meet us outside that little barn. I'll get ours tacked up."

As Liv and Sophie walked away, Sophie grabbed Liv's arm. "That was awful," she whispered. "As if we'd bother with his horses when we have Cisco and Cactus Jack!"

✳ ✳ ✳ ✳ ✳

Sophie leaned forward to straighten Cisco's golden mane as they finally rode out of the Silver Spur corral. "I'm sorry you had to wait for me for so long," she whispered to the ear he swiveled in her direction. "We'll be home soon and I'll have a treat for you. Oats, carrots and maybe an apple."

"Where should we go?" Dayna wheeled Champagne to face the other girls. "Over to Wild Horse Creek? Up to Eagle Nest Mesa?"

"Let's go pay a call on Shane," Cheyenne suggested. Both she and Hailey were riding Silver Spur palominos. Their saddles were beautifully tooled leather and the spurs shiny silver.

Sophie and Liv exchanged glances. Sophie knew that Shane lived in an old trailer, but they had never seen it. Shane was pretty shy about his home life. He might not like five girls on horseback showing up on his doorstep.

26

Still, Sophie thought, *it would be a chance to tell Shane about the coyote in the canyon and Bando's narrow escape. Maybe he'd want to move the herd today.*

"Or is Shane over at your place –?" Cheyenne asked, the curiosity blazing in her face. "I hear he spends a lot of time on the ranch since you girls arrived."

"He spends a lot of time there since Gran and Granddad have been away in Tucson," Liv said sharply. "Mom and Sophie and I don't know much about ranching, and Shane does."

"But he's not there now," Sophie added. "He went to town on an errand for Mom and then he was going home." The town was a small village called Rattlesnake Bend. Around it were small plots of land, many of them with trailers like Shane's.

"So what are we waitin' for? We'll dig that lonesome coyote out of his hole and see if we can get him to come for a ride with us." Dayna clucked to Champagne and set off at a lope down the sandy lane that led from the ranch.

What do these girls want with Shane? Sophie wondered, reluctantly urging Cisco after them. She knew Dayna liked Shane – did Hailey and Cheyenne have crushes on him, too, even though Cheyenne was related to him?

Why not? she thought despairingly as they jogged along the Silver Spur lane. *They're both closer to Shane's age than I am. They go to high school with him. How can I compete?*

Both she and Liv were out of their league, she realized. There was a huge gulf between thirteen and sixteen. She had the feeling this whole day had been planned to size them up and maybe to put them in their place. Pale little know-nothings from "up north." The way Dayna had spat out those words, it was clear that "up north" was no place she'd ever want to go.

Sophie thought longingly of the cool green of Vancouver, the towering trees, the lush gardens, the spring showers that brought everything to life. Here the dry land seemed to stretch on forever to mountain ranges that rose suddenly from the desert, shimmering in the heat. Dust rising from the lane made Sophie's eyes sting.

✵ ✵ ✵ ✵ ✵

"Yee-haw!" With a loud whoop, Dayna urged Champagne into a gallop. She sped away down the red sand road with Hailey and Cheyenne at her heels. "Come on, Champagne," she yelled, "show those Spanish horses your dust."

"Show-off," muttered Liv. She let Cactus Jack have his head. He didn't need any other encouragement. The chestnut flew into an effortless gallop and chased the three horses ahead of him. Liv could hear the steady thud of Cisco's hooves as he thundered behind. For a second, she could feel Sophie's fear – how she'd hate riding at that speed. Then the joy of riding a galloping horse drove everything else from Liv's mind.

Minutes later they raced through the open Silver Spur

gate. Cactus plants and thorn bushes flashed by on either side. Dust rose in a cloud, hiding the horses in front of Liv and filling her eyes and nose.

Riding blind! This was exciting but dangerous. Liv couldn't see the road under Cactus Jack's flying feet. The taste of sand, gritty and bitter, was in her mouth. "Easy, Jack," she cried, trying to slow him with her voice and hands. But Cactus Jack had the bit in his teeth and was not slowing down for anybody.

Liv thrilled to her horse's pounding hoofs, his muscles bunching and reaching under her. He was gaining on the other horses. As they rode into the dust cloud a scream pierced the dust in front of her. Cactus Jack swerved violently, almost throwing her over his shoulder. She heard Sophie's choked shout from behind, "Liv! What's happening?"

The horses came to a halt in a scrambled tangle. At the center a horse was down. As the dust settled Liv saw Dayna's palomino, Flash Dance, stretched on his side. Hailey, covered in dust, lay near him, clutching her shoulder.

Dayna came riding back through the dust cloud. She threw herself off Champagne. "Flash!" She rushed to the horse's side.

Liv and Cheyenne helped Hailey to her feet. The blonde girl's tears made two crooked tracks down her dusty cheeks. "Never mind about your father's fancy show horse," she sobbed. "I think my shoulder's dislocated."

CHAPTER 4
Shane at Home

With Dayna's urging, Flash Dance heaved himself to his feet. He gave a mighty shake and tossed his golden head as if to say, "What was that all about?"

Dayna led him forward a few steps to make sure he wasn't limping. She ran her hands over his withers, back and legs, brushing off the dust, making sure there were no other injuries.

"Whew!" she exclaimed. "I think he's all right."

"You're not even worried about me!" Hailey moaned, clutching her shoulder.

Dayna ignored her complaining. "Any idea what made him go down?"

"I – I think it was a rabbit. Something dashed right in front of us." Hailey stared at Dayna. "Flash Dance went head over heels."

"You were lucky," Liv exclaimed. "But we'd better get you to a doctor."

"I can't ride." Hailey shook her head. "It hurts too much."

"We're just over the hill from Shane's trailer." Cheyenne squinted up the road. "We were headed there anyway and Shane's dad has a truck. Maybe he can drive us into town."

"Can you make it that far?" Dayna asked.

"I guess so." Hailey's face twisted with pain.

As they led their horses behind the three palominos, Sophie found herself shaking with shock and anger. She hugged Cisco's sweaty, dusty neck to steady herself. "That was insane riding," she hissed to Liv. "Why did we have to race?"

"We would have been fine without the dust." Liv took off her hat and banged it against her knee. "Maybe a little reckless, but Cactus Jack and Cisco love to gallop."

"I never thought of Dayna as the reckless type." Sophie glared at Liv. "And you could see how upset she was about hurting one of her dad's horses. Why did she do it?"

Liv shook her head. "Trying to prove her palominos are faster than our Spanish horses, maybe?" She grinned. "I guess we showed her! Cactus Jack would have been in front if I'd really let him go."

"How can you even say that! What if it had been him or Cisco that fell? They could have been really hurt!"

With Hailey groaning all the way, they plodded to the top of a rise from where they could gaze down on Shane's trailer.

"It's sure nuthin' to look at," Cheyenne sighed as they headed down the slope toward it.

The aluminum Airstream trailer shone like a silver bubble in a shimmering stretch of desert. There were no trees or even tall bushes around it; just a small corral, a run-in shed and a pile of hay bales. They could see Shane's buckskin paint Navajo flicking his tail at the flies in the shade of the shed roof.

What a lonesome place to live, Sophie thought as they rode up to the trailer. It was only because nothing ever rotted in the desert that it was still in one piece. The wheels were gone and it was propped up on crossed wooden timbers. A big old satellite dish sat in the yard, along with a dented pickup.

Sophie swallowed hard, thinking of Shane living there with just his father who traveled a lot. No wonder he liked to hang out at the ranch. Her grandparents, Ted and Sandra Starr, were like family to him.

They all stood for a moment, holding their horses. "What are we waitin' for?" Dayna said finally, walking toward the door with a swing of her hips. "Ready or not, Shane Tripp, I'm a-comin' knockin'."

She banged hollowly on the trailer door. There was no answer. Dayna turned with a puzzled shrug. "I can hear Shane's in there and there's someone with him. Wonder why he doesn't come to the door?"

She pounded louder.

Hailey's voice quavered, "Maybe he just doesn't want anybody botherin' him."

"Horse feathers! Your shoulder's messed up and we've

got to get you to town." Dayna pounded again. "Come on, Shane, we know you're in there."

The trailer door opened. Shane's fair head, hatless, poked out. When he saw the five girls he stared, then came down the narrow steps, his black-and-white dog Tux at his heels.

He gave Sophie an embarrassed glance. "I thought you were goin' to the Silver Spur s-spa," he stammered.

"We were," Sophie said. "But –"

"We wanted to come pay you a visit and on the way we had a little accident," Dayna finished her sentence.

"Hailey's hurt, Shane." Cheyenne walked up to the tall thin cowboy and peered at him from under the brim of her hat. "She can't ride. Can you drive her to the clinic in Rattlesnake Bend?"

Shane stared at Hailey's woeful face. "I-uh-sure. I just don't know if I've got enough gas to get to Rattlesnake Bend and back. Let me go and get some cash." He fled back inside.

They heard shouting and then Shane was back, slamming the door behind him. "All right!" He sounded almost angry. "Let's go. Who's comin' with me?"

"I'll come along with you and Hailey," Cheyenne said. With Hailey still gripping her arm, the two girls and Shane climbed in the cab of the pickup without a backward glance. Tux leaped into the back. The truck took off in a cloud of dust.

Sophie gazed after it. Shane hadn't seemed like the

same person they knew – not at all. What was wrong and who was in the trailer?"

Dayna picked up the reins of Champagne and the other Silver Spur horses. She peered at Liv and Sophie over the tops of her sunglasses. "Listen, you two. It would be faster to turn around on this road and take the first cut off to your ranch than to ride all the way back to my place and go home through Wild Horse Creek Canyon. D'you think you might be able to find your way?"

"Of course we can," Liv told her. "Guess we'll have to have that lunch and massage some other time."

"Sure thing." Dayna promised. She flashed Liv a wicked grin. "I'll say hi to Temo for you." She mounted Champagne in one smooth motion and rode away, leading the other horses.

Heading off in the opposite direction, Sophie squirmed in her saddle as if a burr of jealousy was stuck under her jeans. Did Shane just forget about her when he was with Cheyenne and Hailey? She hadn't had a chance to tell him about the coyote's attack on Diego's colt. He could at least have said goodbye instead of speeding off that way in his truck. She'd never seen him drive. Up to now he'd always appeared at the Lucky Star Ranch riding Navajo.

I like him a hundred times better on horseback, Sophie thought.

Shane had seemed much friendlier when he thought they were leaving, she suddenly realized. Recently he'd been acting strange and stand-offish. Had she done something to offend him? Or was he just backing away because he knew she was staying at the Lucky Star for months?

She didn't share these thoughts with Liv. At one time she'd confided everything to her twin, but now Sophie had feelings she didn't want to share with anyone.

I wonder when I'll see Shane again? she asked herself, *and how will he act when I do?*

✳ ✳ ✳ ✳ ✳

As they rode into the Lucky Star ranch yard an hour later, Liv wished she hadn't mentioned Temo to Dayna.

She's going to tease him about me, for sure, Liv thought *and he'll be embarrassed and think I'm a dumb little kid.*

Liv remembered the first time she had seen Temo. He was more handsome than Shane, she decided, with chiseled lips, a straight nose and flashing dark eyes full of laughter. Where Shane was thin as a desert fence post, Temo was solid – strong, but tender underneath.

She remembered how he had risked his job at the Silver Spur to help them save their grandparents' horses, how he had brought them blankets and food when they were hiding on the ranch, how he smiled when he called her *muchacha*, little girl, how he rode like the wind on his black-and-white paint horse, so at home in this big wild country.

She wondered about his life – why he stayed on

working for Sam Regis when he didn't like or respect him. His family worked there; that was part of the reason, she knew. She had been hoping to find out more about him at lunch today.

"I'm glad we didn't have to stay for lunch." Sophie slipped from Cisco's saddle in front of the low wooden barn. "I didn't want to face Dayna's father again."

Liv dismounted with a sigh. As usual, she and Sophie had been thinking about the same thing in totally different ways. Sophie hated the thought of lunch at the Silver Spur, while Liv was longing for the chance to see Temo and his family.

It was as if she and Sophie were two sides of the same coin.

Back home in Vancouver they'd cruised along in the same class at school with the same friends and the same dance teachers and the same ski club, she thought as they led the two horses into the cool dim barn. Here it was as if the bright desert sun shone a spotlight on everything that made them different.

I love the wide-open spaces, Liv thought, *and they make Sophie nervous. I like the sun, and she misses big trees and shade. I want to take risks and have adventures. She likes to play it safe. It's like we're strangers all of a sudden.*

Arizona had brought them closer together, in only one way she could see.

Before, Liv thought, *I was the one who loved horses. Sophie rode, but her heart wasn't in it.*

But as they groomed Cactus Jack and Cisco after their ride, Liv watched Sophie brush every speck of dust and sweat from Cisco's hide, check his feet for stones, and feed him oats and carrots.

"You've come a long way," Liv said. "You never cared about the riding stable horses back home."

"Those horses weren't Cisco," Sophie grinned.

They led Cisco and Cactus Jack to the corral, slipped off their halters and watched them sink gratefully to the ground and roll like two large puppies in the sand. "There goes all our hard work." Liv laughed. "Dirty as ever."

"Cisco's wonderful," Sophie said. "I can trust him. We're on the same wavelength. Maybe he wasn't a special horse till I started riding him. Maybe I wasn't a very good rider. But together we're good."

CHAPTER 5
Mexican Food

Sophie woke next morning from a crazy dream where Shane rode into the Lucky Star ranch yard, leaped from Navajo's back, swept her into his arms and kissed her. She'd never had dreams like this before and they made her want to leap out of bed, tear downstairs, jump on Cisco and ride off across the desert.

Instead she waited at the ranch gate. The Lucky Star cap gate was decorated with a big L and a star. Below it was a barred gate that swung open on hinges. Sophie leaned against it, watching for spurts of dust far down the road that meant Navajo and Shane were coming.

Instead, a large plume of dust appeared in the distance. A car or truck, Sophie thought as it came closer. It was Shane. Sophie hurried to swing the gate open for the battered pickup they'd seen at his trailer.

Choking from fumes and dust she closed the gate after

the truck and ran to meet Shane as he climbed out of the cab. "Where's Navajo?" Sophie gazed up at his face.

"Don't want to talk about it." Shane barely glanced at her as he headed for the kitchen where her mom, Jess, was cooking bacon and eggs. Jess Winchester was slim and dark like her twin daughters and looked perfectly at home in the ranch house where she had grown up.

Shane took off his hat and stood in the kitchen door, leaving Tux outside, whining to get in.

"Breakfast?" Jess Winchester turned from the large gas range to ask.

"Don't bother, I'm fine." Shane waved his hat. "But I have a favor to ask, ma'am."

"Ask away." Jess turned back to her frying pan.

"I can work here on the ranch steady this week. It's our spring break. And I was wonderin' if I could get an advance on my pay."

"Sure. No problem."

"It's just that our electric bill's come due and my dad hasn't been workin' much lately."

"You don't have to explain." Jess lifted the eggs out of the pan and slid them on a plate with three pieces of bacon. "You're keeping the Lucky Star going almost single-handedly, Shane. Anything we can do to help is our pleasure. Have some breakfast – before it gets cold."

It might have been Shane's dad that they'd heard in the trailer, Sophie realized. The shouting might have been about money. As Shane headed for ranch house's big main room, she grabbed a piece of toast from the toaster, slathered it with butter and followed him to the dining table.

"Thanks." Shane took the toast without looking up.

"I'd like to talk to you about Diego and the herd," Sophie began. "Something happened yesterday –"

Just then, Liv came pounding down the stairs. "Hey Shane," she sang out. "You're later than usual. Why is Tux outside?" She danced to the front door to let him in. Tux dashed under the table and lay with his head on his outstretched paws, gazing up at his master.

"I didn't mean to stay for breakfast," said Shane.

"I don't see why not. You always have breakfast here." Liv's round brown eyes were brimming with curiosity. "Did you hear any more about Hailey's shoulder?"

Shane gulped down a bite of bacon. "Nope. I dropped her and Cheyenne at the clinic. Hailey called her folks on her cell. They were meetin' her there."

Sophie grabbed Liv's arm. "Let Shane finish while we help Mom in the kitchen."

"What's wrong with him?" Liv hissed when the kitchen door had swung shut. "He looks as miserable as a horse without hay."

"It's none of our business," Sophie told her, "and he doesn't want to talk about it."

"Hmpf!" Liv tossed up her shoulders. "Things seem a lot easier if you talk them out – and we're his friends. Have you told him about the coyote in the canyon yet?"

"I haven't had a chance," Sophie said. "I was just about to tell him when you interrupted."

"Well come on, let's do it now." Liv grabbed her arm and propelled her back to the dining room, but as Sophie sat down beside Shane the phone rang.

Liv rushed to answer it. "Hi Dayna," Sophie heard her say. "Today? Sure we'll come. What time? Okay. He will? That's great."

Sophie was shaking her head furiously but it was too late. Liv plunked down the phone with a huge grin on her face.

"Dayna rescheduled our lunch. Temo's going to pick us up at twelve." She sat down with a happy shrug of her shoulders. "I said we'd be ready."

"I heard," Sophie grumbled. "I wish you hadn't said yes for me. I don't want to go back to the Silver Spur Spa. What will Dayna's father say if he sees us again?"

"Oh stop being such a little black cloud. It'll be fun." Liv threw her arms wide as if embracing the day to come.

"Shane might need us today," Sophie looked pleadingly at the young cowboy.

"Don't need you." Shane kept his head down, chewing steadily, the muscles in his thin face working.

He might as well have said he doesn't want us, Sophie thought. "Shane," she gulped, "Diego's foal ran into a coyote yesterday and almost got caught. Carmelita chased him away, but I wondered –"

"I'll go check on the herd today," Shane interrupted.

"Want to find the gap in the fence where Sam Regis let his horses through the other week. If he thinks he can get away with it again, he'll use the spring in the canyon to water his stock."

"But I thought, maybe if the canyon's so dangerous, we should bring the herd in," Sophie faltered.

Shane gave her a glance that clearly said she didn't know what she was talking about. "It's important to have Diego and his herd out there," he explained patiently. "That's the best way to keep off all those ranchers who are tryin' to force your Granddad to sell his land and the spring."

"I wish I could go with you, to check on them," Sophie said in a low voice.

"Well you can't." Liv grabbed her by the arm and swung her up from the table. "We're going to lunch."

✳ ✳ ✳ ✳ ✳

The ride to Silver Spur, sitting beside Temo, was too short.

It isn't as if he treats me like anything special, Liv thought. *He's as friendly and charming to Sophie as he is to me.*

It was just the way his shoulders bunched when he steered the truck around a corner, and the way his black hair, cut short, made a perfect curve around his ears, and the glint of laughter that was always in his eyes, not like he was laughing at *them,* but like he saw the lighter side of life.

"I'll see you." He smiled as he let them out of the truck. "Enjoy your lunch, *muchachas*."

The dining area of the Silver Spur guest ranch was decorated in western style, like the spa. A low roof of woven grass called a *ramada* sheltered an open courtyard. On one side was an enormous stone barbecue and oven. Bright flowering bushes screened the other sides. Round wrought iron tables with matching chairs were set on a terra cotta tile floor. Brightly colored tablecloths covered them and metal lanterns with rearing horses cut into them sat in the center of each table. On the napkin rings were more running horses.

"Where did Temo go?" Liv asked Dayna as they took their places around the table. There was a sprinkling of other guests at the tables, most of them well-groomed older women.

"Back to the barns, I guess." Dayna raised one well-shaped eyebrow.

"Isn't he going to have lunch?" Liv pressed.

"He doesn't eat in here – with us," Dayna said. She looked down her nose at Liv. "The help eats in the kitchen, not with the guests."

"Oh." Liv shared a glance with Sophie. "That's too bad. Maybe some of the guests would like to meet the real cowboys who work here."

"Maybe." Dayna lifted her chin. "But I'm sure Temo is more comfortable with his own people. His mother's our cook."

"You might be right." Liv looked around. "He probably *is* more at home with his family than with a bunch of stuffy old snobs." The remark popped out of her mouth before she could stop it. She glanced at Sophie who was shaking her head.

Dayna flushed red under her tan. Her angry outburst was stalled by the appearance of a stunningly pretty server wearing a swirling western skirt, a red cowboy shirt and broad-brimmed hat slung against her back.

Before they could order, Cheyenne and Hailey came hurrying toward the table. Hailey wore a sling to hold her sore shoulder in position. "Sorry we're late," she apologized. "It takes so long to get this thing on." She raised her elbow and winced. "The doc said I can't ride for another two weeks."

While they pulled out chairs and sat down, Dayna ordered for them in rapid Spanish. Showing off again, Liv thought. She was so disappointed in not seeing Temo that she didn't feel like eating. Was the gorgeous server someone he worked with every day?

Lunch arrived quickly. Again Sophie and Liv shared a glance. They recognized the green glop next to the corn chips – that was *guacamole* – made from avocados. The tacos and beans looked familiar. But what, Liv wondered, was that slab of stuff that looked like boiled cardboard? She picked up her knife and fork and tried to cut off a piece.

Loud bursts of laughter erupted from Dayna and her friends.

"That's a corn husk, " Hailey giggled. "You can't cut through it. You unfold it, like this." She deftly flipped the corn husk over and folded back the ends to reveal a steaming center of cornmeal, cheese and green chilies.

"It's a *tamale,*" Cheyenne explained. "Haven't you ever had one before?"

Liv and Sophie shook their heads. "You'll like it," Cheyenne promised. "Try it."

There was silence as the twins struggled to open their *tamales* and took bites. "You're right," Sophie gasped. "This is delicious."

"Yum!" Liv added.

"You should see your faces," laughed Hailey. "Exactly the same expression on both of them. You might not be identical but you're twins, for sure."

"There's an art to making real Mexican *tamales*," Dayna said proudly. "The Silver Spur serves the best in Southern Arizona."

No mention of the fact that Temo's mother made them, thought Liv.

There were deep-fried ice cream and chocolate cookies for dessert. Every time the kitchen door swung open, Liv tried to catch a glimpse of Temo or his mother, but a large flowering hibiscus blocked her view.

"Should we offer to pay for the lunch?" Sophie whispered while the others were laughing at one of Cheyenne's jokes.

"No. This was part of our gift day at the spa, remember?" Liv tried to peer around the flowering tree.

"Well, we should at least thank Dayna for such a delicious meal," Sophie nudged her.

"You do it, then." Liv was still angry about not seeing Temo.

"This has been great," Sophie said to Dayna at last, "but we should get back to the Lucky Star. I want to help Shane this afternoon."

"Is he at your place again?" Cheyenne looked surprised. "After all the trouble he's had I thought he'd stay home."

"He came in the truck," Sophie said quickly. "What trouble?"

Cheyenne hesitated. "Maybe I shouldn't talk about it," she said. "My stepmother is Shane's aunt so I get all the gossip."

Liv and Sophie shared another look. Her *stepmother*! So Shane and Cheyenne weren't actually related, except by marriage.

CHAPTER 6
Double Trouble

"Oh, come on, Cheyenne." Dayna tossed her head. "You can't keep a secret in a small place like Rattlesnake Bend. Everybody knows Shane's dad Harlan went on a bender last week and lost his licence for drunk drivin'. Shane most likely took the truck so his dad couldn't get his hands on it. He's probably scared his dad will try to drive."

Liv watched Sophie's face turn pale. Now she'd be more anxious than ever to get home and see Shane. Liv hoped Temo would drive them back, but Dayna's mother, Brenda, dressed in a white linen pantsuit, slid behind the wheel of the red truck. She looked exactly like an older version of Dayna, Liv thought, blonde hair swooped up, elegantly manicured hands on the steering wheel.

"You gals have a good time?" she drawled.

"The food was delicious," Liv said. This at least was the truth.

"Well, I'm glad," said Brenda Regis. "We like to be friendly to our neighbors."

Shane had already gone home by the time they arrived at the Lucky Star. "He said he had to look after his horse," Jess told them as they waved goodbye to the Silver Spur pickup.

The two girls went to check Cisco and Cactus Jack. Shane had filled their water trough and brought hay for their evening feed. The horses stood in the shade of a live oak tree, nose to tail.

"Cisco looks perfectly happy," Sophie sighed. "Shane's taken care of everything. I wish I could have talked to him."

"Don't worry, he'll be back tomorrow." Liv leaned on the corral fence, watching the horses swish the flies off each others' backs. "Maybe then he'll open up about his dad."

"Some people don't like to talk about their troubles." Their mother Jess had joined them at the corral fence. "Shane reminds me of your brother Mark in that way."

At the mention of their sixteen-year-old brother, Liv and Sophie shared a look of longing and regret. Mark was in Vancouver, living with their dad and his girlfriend. They knew their mom missed him badly. They all did.

"Do you think Mark will ever come down here?" Liv asked, putting her arm around her mother's waist.

"Who knows?" Jess shrugged. "Maybe – if we're still here in the summer when he's out of school."

That night there was a call from their grandfather in Tucson. They all talked to him on extensions of the ranch phone.

"Sandra's surgery is scheduled for tomorrow." Ted Starr's voice sounded as gravelly and rough as the man himself. "So that's all settled. How are things there? How's my horse – how's Diego?"

"Fine," all three of them chorused.

"Be sure to keep him close to the ranch till he's strong again," Ted advised. "It's too risky lettin' the herd range along Wild Horse Creek – too many cougars. Can't risk losing another foal."

There was so much Granddad didn't know, Sophie thought guiltily. He didn't know about the mystery stallion stealing Carmelita and the other mares and foals. He didn't know about Sam Regis trying to ship his horses away. And there was no use telling him any of this. He had enough worries with Gran being sick and having an operation.

"How are you, Pop?" their mother asked.

"Well, I'd be all right if I could get some fresh air," Granddad grumbled. "This here motel and all them doctors' offices got the windows sealed up and the danged air conditioning blasting. A man can't breathe."

"I'll look on the net and see if I can find a motel where the windows open, Granddad," Sophie promised. She could imagine how her grandfather would feel cooped up in airless rooms in a big city. There was no air conditioning on the Lucky Star ranch house. At night, the desert air was always cool and they slept with the windows open. During the hot days, the thick adobe walls kept the house comfortable.

"Thank you, child," Granddad said. "Take good care of yourself and say hello to Shane for us."

If Shane's talking to us tomorrow, Sophie thought as she hung up the phone.

She twisted a strand of her fine hair around her finger in an anxious gesture. What would Granddad think if he knew Diego and the herd were out along Wild Horse Creek at this moment? "Mom," she blurted out, "we should do what Granddad said and bring the horses up close to the barn."

"I agree," Jess nodded. "But we can't do that by ourselves. We'll have to wait for Shane."

✳ ✳ ✳ ✳ ✳

They waited for hours the next morning, but Shane didn't appear. Sophie and Liv fed and watered the horses and cleaned their tack and saddles, not wanting to leave the barn in case he came.

Finally, when it was nearly noon, they heard Tux's sharp bark and saw the black-and-white dog trotting down the ranch lane. Behind him walked Shane, leading a limping Navajo. Shane's hat was pulled so far down his forehead they could hardly see his eyes. His mouth was a grim line. He threw a rope around the veranda rail and stomped inside the ranch house without stopping to talk to them.

52

"Ma'am?" he said to Jess, who was sitting doing bills at Ted Starr's big oak desk, "I need a place to board my horse."

"We've got plenty of room in the barn," said Jess, looking up in surprise.

"I'll be stayin' in Rattlesnake Bend, with my aunt," Shane went on, "but she's got no place to keep a horse."

"It's no problem," Liv said. She and Sophie had followed Shane into the room. "You know Navajo's welcome here."

"What happened, Shane?" Sophie gulped. "Was it something about your dad?"

"Cheyenne filled us in yesterday at lunch," Liv confessed. "We know about him losing his licence."

Shane slumped into a chair and took off his hat. "I guess you might as well hear the whole story, then," he muttered. He looked up, his gray-blue eyes full of pain. "Yesterday when I got back to the trailer I found out he'd been tryin' to ride Navajo, 'cause I took his truck, I guess. Navajo tossed him off and then Pa beat him, and that's why I wasn't able to ride out here this mornin'." He felt in his pocket. "I took Pa's keys so he can't drive unless he hot-wires the truck and I guess that's all I can do."

"You don't have to stay in town," Liv said. "You could sleep in Gran's and Granddad's room until they get back."

"No, I couldn't do that." Shane shook his head violently. "Wouldn't be respectful."

"There's a bunkhouse near the barn," Sophie pointed through the window. "You could move in there."

53

"That's an excellent idea." Jess beamed. "At least for this week while you're not in school."

"I don't like to put my troubles on you." Shane shook his head again. "Never know what Pa's likely to do."

"We'll share our troubles," Jess said gently. "The girls' grandfather called, and he thinks we should bring the horses up to the ranch. I agree, especially after the girls told me about the foal being attacked by a coyote yesterday."

"I hear you," Shane said. "I guess I'd better round 'em up and bring 'em in."

Jess nodded. "Take Cactus Jack or Cisco for now. When you bring in the herd, choose another horse to ride till Navajo is better."

"You can take Cactus Jack," Liv volunteered. "Then Sophie can go with you."

Sometimes Sophie felt as if Liv really did understand her, after all. Liv loved riding Cactus Jack in the desert, and she was giving her a chance to be alone with Shane.

✻ ✻ ✻ ✻ ✻

"Darling Navajo," Liv whispered in the tan-and-gold paint's ear after Sophie and Shane had ridden away. "How could anyone mistreat you?" Navajo stood in the shade of the live oak tree, looking fixedly at the spot where the two riders had disappeared.

Liv imagined how angry Shane must have been to find Navajo beaten and limping. Shane had got his horse from the Navajo tribe up at the four corners where Arizona,

New Mexico, Colorado and Idaho met. It was a special place and the horses bred on Native American lands were tough, sturdy and most of all intelligent. Navajo was more than just a dependable ride to Shane. The horse was his loyal companion, his best friend.

It's people who let you down, not animals, Liv thought bitterly. People like Shane's dad, and her own father. Their dad had announced last Christmas that he was leaving the family and moving in with another woman, and Liv had felt her trust in people tottering ever since. *Maybe it happens to everyone when they get to be thirteen*, she thought. *You realize not every adult is worth your respect, let alone your love.*

"Don't worry, we'll give you the best treatment a horse ever had," promised Liv. "Shane will be back riding you before you know it."

✳ ✳ ✳ ✳ ✳

"Which horse will you pick to ride from the herd?" Sophie glanced at Shane, trying to make conversation. She and Shane had ridden side by side all the way to Wild Horse Creek without exchanging a single word.

Shane carried a rope coiled in his hand. Tux trotted at his side. "I'm thinkin' about a little mare called Trixie," he told Sophie. "She doesn't have a foal this year and she's fast and well-trained."

"How hard will it be to bring in the herd?" asked Sophie.

"Harder for me than it would be for your grandfather."

Shane hitched up his shoulders. It was easier for him to talk about horses than his personal problems. "He and Diego have an understandin'. Diego knows Ted won't do his bunch any harm and he'll let them run free soon as he can. Back when this ranch ran hundreds of head of cattle, all the horses got used regular. Now not so often." He looked down at his dog. "You ready to work, Tux?" he asked.

The border collie gave an eager yelp.

"Between this good cuttin' horse and this good herdin' dog we should have no problem," Shane said. "You can ride alongside and make sure there ain't no strays."

Sophie gulped. She was frightened, but exhilarated at the chance to help Shane. "There they are," she cried. "Just where we saw them yesterday."

The stallion, Diego, wove in and out among his mares, his tail high, his neck arched, on the alert. "Yesterday he stood up on that bluff, watching over the herd like a king." Sophie pointed. "Today he seems worried about something."

"Likely knows we're roundin' up his band," Shane said. "That little bay with the white markings is Trixie." He urged Cactus Jack into a fast jog. "Let's go get 'em, pardner."

"Wait!" Sophie had been scanning the canyon floor. "Where's Carmelita and her foal? Bando – that's what Liv and I decided to call him yesterday – at least until Gran can give him a real name."

"They should be somewhere around here," Shane turned to look. "She's the lead mare – never far from Diego."

"I know, but that colt's a wanderer with a mind of his own. Maybe he didn't learn his lesson yesterday and he's run off up Coyote Canyon again."

"Well, c'mon. We'll take a look." Shane wore a worried frown as he swung up on Cactus Jack and led the way with Tux. Sophie followed, searching every bit of the canyon sides for the sight of a shiny sorrel mane or a black bottlebrush tail.

CHAPTER 7
Death in the Desert

Black birds circled in the dazzling blue desert sky as
Sophie and Shane neared a bend in the canyon far from
the Lucky Star herd.

Vultures! Sophie knew that these soaring black birds
meant only one thing. Something had died in the desert –
or was dying.

Her throat was dry as she urged Cisco forward. What
had the vultures found?

Around the bend the canyon of Wild Horse Creek
narrowed under overhanging boulders and ledges of
rock. Below the rocks, red, orange and yellow spring
wildflowers lit the narrow canyon floor.

A glint of darker red among the cactus blossoms
caught Sophie's eye. Choking back her fear, she rode
closer. Cisco's hoofs crunched over the rough, sandy soil.

The sun slanting off canyon walls blinded her and the hum of insects buzzed in her ears.

She heard Tux growl and glanced down. The dog was pressed to the desert sand, his hackles raised. His sharp nose pointed to the reddish shape that was partly hidden by tall branching cactii. She rode closer. There was no mistaking it – it was the body of a horse.

"Oh, no," Sophie gasped. "Carmelita!"

Shane caught up to her, slipped from Cactus Jack's back and handed his reins to Sophie. "Stay here." He strode toward Carmelita's body. "Keep the horses back," he said in a low voice. "They can spook at the smell of death. You stay back too, Tux."

Sophie knew Shane was shielding her from the worst of the sight in front of them. Even from here she could see that there had been a terrible struggle and Carmelita had lost.

"It must have been a cougar – a mountain lion." Shane straightened up from the gruesome remains of what had been a beautiful horse. "The mare's throat is torn in the way cougars kill."

"Poor Carmelita," Sophie mourned. "She could fight off a coyote but not a mountain lion. But she must have fought with all her strength to save her foal. Can you see the colt?"

"No sign of him here."

"How long ago," she gulped, "do you think it happened?"

"Maybe a few hours." Shane looked up at the circling vultures. "The birds have already been at work."

Sophie felt a wave of nausea overwhelm her. Vultures always went for the eyes first. She clutched Cactus Jack's reins in one hand, her saddle horn in the other. She must not faint, or be sick. That wasn't going to help Bando. He wasn't lying there next to his mother, so there was still hope that he'd gotten away.

"We'll have to look for the colt," she told Shane. "He might be the hope of the herd. He looks like his father, and when Diego is too old to be the boss stallion, Bando might take over. And with Carmelita gone, there will never be another foal like him." The words rushed out of her.

"It's no use, Sophie." Shane shoved back his hat and stared up at the canyon walls. His face was thin and strained. "The cat probably dragged the poor little guy off with him. It'd feed on the colt first and then come back for the mare. It could be anywhere up in those rocks."

Tux was nosing around the brush near Carmelita's body. "Get away from there, Tux," ordered Shane. "We have to get the rest of the herd in before we lose any more horses."

"I'm going to look anyway," Sophie insisted. "I have to find out what happened to Bando." She wasn't going to break down – wasn't going to cry until she knew for sure, until she saw with her own eyes that the colt was dead. She thought of their promise to her grandmother to look after the horses while she was away. How could they let Gran down so totally and how could they say, "We think his bones are somewhere on the side of the canyon, but we don't know for sure"?

It wasn't good enough.

Tux had stopped sniffing and had started to bark.

"Cut that out, you crazy dog," scolded Shane. "We're leavin'."

Sophie held Cactus Jack's reins out to Shane. "Here. You go and get the herd in. I'm going to stay and look."

Shane grabbed the reins from her hand. "You and your sister are so dang stubborn, it makes me crazy. Think about what you're dealing with here – a full-grown cougar with its prey – you don't just go marching up to it and interfere. Maybe you should take a look at what its teeth and claws did to Carmelita. Sophie! Are you listenin' to me?"

"I hear you," Sophie murmured. "I'm sorry if I seem stubborn, but I have to know." Tux was still barking, his yelps echoing off the canyon walls.

"You have to know – *you have to know*," Shane raged as he marched off to collect his dog. "Dumb greenhorn."

It was the harshest name Shane had ever called her. A greenhorn was the butt of all jokes among cowboys – the person who didn't know one end of a horse from the other. The insult stung but it didn't change things. In her mind Sophie could still see Bando frisking up the creek bed, his bottlebrush tail waving like a flag, full of energy and life.

Shane was yelling at his dog. "Tux! What are you barkin' at?"

"We might not be too l-late." Sophie urged Cisco forward. "We might still be able to save Bando."

"Wait, Sophie." Shane was bent over near Tux, staring at the ground.

"What is it?" Had Tux found Bando's body near his mother, after all? Sophie rode back and slid from her saddle. She stood, holding Cisco's reins, frozen.

"Tie him up and come here," Shane called. "It's not the colt – it's the cougar."

✷ ✷ ✷ ✷ ✷

At that moment Liv was driving into town with her mother in the Lucky Star ranch truck.

Rattlesnake Bend straggled across the top of a hill, surrounded by steep mountain ranges. It had a boot hill – a cemetery where cowboys and gamblers, rustlers and outlaws from the old days were buried with wood crosses to mark their graves. The main street was lined with old wood buildings that had once been saloons and boarding houses for the cowboys who brought their herds through Rattlesnake Bend on their way to the railway to the north. Now they housed stores and businesses.

Surrounding the old town and trailing down the hill to the west were new developments – plazas and housing – as well as the regional schools.

"Next week!" Liv shuddered as they drove past the high wire fence surrounding the Rattlesnake Bend Junior

High School. "Sophie and I will be spending all our days in that building."

The Winchesters had agreed to stay in Arizona till the end of the school year and perhaps longer. At least until Gran was on her feet.

"It won't be so bad," her mother promised. "Don't forget I went to that school."

"A billion years ago."

Jess laughed and reached over to pat Liv's knee. "Not quite that long. Anyway, when were you ever scared of something new?"

"Now!" Liv leaned her chin on her hand and stared out the truck window. "I'm not sure the kids here are going to accept us."

Her mother pulled into a parking place in front of the drug store. The main street in Rattlesnake Bend was so wide the parking spaces slanted toward the sidewalk. "Why do you say that?" she asked, looking sharply at Liv. This was usually Sophie's role – to be full of fears about the future – not bold, confident Liv.

"Because I'm in culture shock here," Liv burst out. "We come from so far away I don't pick up the local signals. Dayna and her friends laughed at me when I tried to cut into a *tamale*, and because I didn't know what a barrel race was. It seems like as long as Sophie and I were just visiting for a couple of weeks we were okay, but now that we're going to live in Arizona they've suddenly decided we're weird."

"It won't last long," Jess assured her. "Remind people you're Ted and Sandra Starr's granddaughters. The name means something around here. Now let's get out of this hot truck and do some shopping."

While her mother went to the back of the store to fill a prescription, Liv hung around the front of the store, examining the shelves of sunscreen and skin creams. To her horror, Cheyenne and Hailey caught her right in front of a display of self-tanning lotions.

Hailey was still wearing the shoulder brace. "This one would be just right for you," she said, trying to keep a straight face while holding up a tube that promised instant bronzing.

Liv could see Cheyenne smother a giggle.

"Thanks for the advice," Liv nodded. She could feel her face getting red. "But I'm sure I'll tan naturally. After all I have Mexican ancestors."

This brought a surprised silence. "You do?" Cheyenne asked.

"Sure. My grandmother's great grandmother was Maria Lopez. She and her husband settled this country and built the Lucky Star Ranch." Liv drew her shoulders back proudly. Was this what her mother meant by reminding people about her grandparents? Liv wasn't sure but it seemed to work. Hailey gave her a questioning look, then stuck the bronzing cream back on the shelf and changed the subject.

"Did you know that Shane is moving in with Cheyenne?" she asked, her head tipped to one side.

"Why's that?" Liv pretended innocence.

"Because his aunt is married to my dad, and he needs a place to stay." Cheyenne said with a shrug. "It'll be pretty tight at our place, but we'll manage to squeeze him in somewhere."

"Don't worry," Liv told her. "You won't have to squeeze him in. He's staying in the bunkhouse at the Lucky Star. He's working at our place this week, anyway."

"Oh!" Cheyenne gulped. "But maybe he'd rather stay with relatives – family."

"Maybe," Liv agreed. "He's old enough to make up his own mind where he wants to live." She took a deep breath. "There's my mom. Looks like we'd better get going – got to get back to the ranch and make that bunkhouse nice and cozy – for Shane."

She wished Sophie was there to see the disappointed frown on Cheyenne's face.

"Drop by and see us sometime." Liv waved goodbye "If you're out near the Lucky Star ranch."

"Uh ... sure." Cheyenne gave a fake little wave back. She looked as though she'd just bitten into a lemon, Liv thought to herself, grinning.

"Are those the girls you met at Dayna Regis's spa?" Jess asked as she and Liv left the store.

"The dark one's Cheyenne and the blonde one is Hailey. They're both fifteen." Liv nodded. "I don't think I exactly warmed up our friendship but at least I didn't let them walk all over me."

"Liv!" Her mother stopped walking and stared at her. "What did you say?"

"Not much." Liv grinned again. "I just told them Shane was probably going to stay with us this week and then I invited them to come visit."

"I see." Jess frowned. "But it seems to me Shane has enough troubles right now without a bunch of girls fighting over him."

"I know, Mom, but I couldn't help it," Liv shrugged. "Those girls act like they own him – especially Cheyenne. She claims to be some kind of cousin, but she's not really related to Shane."

"Seriously, Liv. Shane's our friend. I wouldn't want to see him embarrassed."

"Don't worry." Liv shrugged. "I don't think Shane will even notice. He's got more important things to worry about."

CHAPTER 8
Unwanted Help

Shane stood looking down at the cougar. Sophie looped Cisco's reins around a rock and stepped slowly forward.

She tried to prepare herself for a bloody sight, but the mountain lion lay stretched out like a cat asleep on the ground. Its tawny body was almost unmarked.

"Must have been a heck of a battle," Shane muttered. "Carmelita must have stomped on him and kicked him clear over here before her strength left her."

"You sure the lion's dead?" Sophie approached cautiously

"As a doornail." Shane nodded. "He was a young fella. That's likely why Carmelita was able to hold her own."

"Then ... where's the colt?" Sophie choked out the words.

Shane looked up. "He must've dashed outta here like a little bolt of lightning."

"So let's go and find him."

Shane straightened up. "First we take the herd back to the ranch and get a search organized, get some more water and grub," he insisted. "Remember the last time you went out in the desert without a full canteen?"

Sophie knew Shane was right. The last time she'd fallen off Cisco and nearly died of thirst out here. The vultures were circling *her* before Tux and the others had found her. And they had to get Diego's band safely back to the ranch. There might be other cougars around.

"All right, but we have to hurry," she urged. "Bando must be lost and terrified or Tux would have found him by now."

"We'll go as fast as we can," Shane said grimly as he swung up on Cactus Jack's saddle. "Don't want the mares and foals runnin' on this rough ground." He looked hard at Sophie from under the brim of his cowboy hat. "I had no business callin' you a greenhorn," he said. " But this round up is no job for somebody whose nerves ain't steady. Are you sure you're okay to help get those critters to the Lucky Star?"

Sophie shuddered, looking down at the body of the dead cougar. "I'm okay," she gulped. She wasn't sure, but she couldn't let Shane down.

✳ ✳ ✳ ✳ ✳

The coyote who had almost caught Bando two days before lay in the shadow of a boulder watching the herd.

His limp had healed but he stayed around, hoping he'd be luckier the second time.

A little chestnut filly with two white socks had caught his hungry eye. She was only a few weeks old and couldn't run as fast as the others. The coyote watched her constantly with his yellow eyes. The herd was milling around. Maybe it was about to move. Maybe in the confusion he would get his chance for a tasty lunch of horsemeat at last.

The coyote crept from behind his boulder. He was a gray shadow against the desert rocks as he slunk to the shadow of a low-spreading manzanita bush. From there he moved closer, his eyes never leaving his prey, the small reddish foal.

※ ※ ※ ※ ※

"Why doesn't Diego lead?" Sophie called to Shane on the other side of the band as they started up Wild Horse Creek Canyon. The band was a ragged bunch, some mares choosing one path, some another over the rocky ground.

"That's the lead mare's job," Shane called back. "Diego's job is to watch from the rear, keep them movin'."

"They must miss Carmelita."

Shane nodded. "They're spooked without her, that's for sure. We'll talk to them, or sing, calm 'em down as we go."

Sophie nodded, her voice sticking in her throat. She blinked back tears thinking of Carmelita's sacrifice, her poor bloody body lying so still, her foal somewhere out there, if he was alive, searching for her. Why hadn't he returned to the rest of the herd?

She gave Cisco his head, knowing he was a good cow horse, like Cactus Jack. Keeping the herd moving and watching for strays was what he was trained to do. A small chestnut foal lagged behind and Cisco turned back to chase her into line.

"Come on, little girl, you have to catch up," Sophie urged the foal. She caught a blur of motion out of her right eye. A low gray body streaked toward the foal.

"Shane!" Sophie screamed. "It's the coyote!"

Cisco raced forward. Before they could reach the foal another animal, black and white, shot in from the left. It was Tux – barking furiously.

The coyote turned and fled. But the barking and commotion, combined with Sophie's scream, startled the already spooked mares. With one sweeping motion, like birds in flight, they wheeled and galloped straight toward Sophie, not sure what the threat was, but running for their lives in a full stampede.

"Sophie!" she heard Shane's yell above the pounding hoofs. "Get out of the way!"

Sophie couldn't even think of her danger. All she saw were the frightened foals and their mothers running too fast on that dangerous ground. In her mind's eye she saw broken legs and trampled bodies. She grabbed the hat from her head and clutched the saddle horn.

"Yee-haw!" Shouting at the top of her lungs and waving her hat Sophie and Cisco turned the herd of fleeing mares. On the other side, Diego and Shane did the rest, slowing the mare in front, breaking the momentum of the stampede.

In seconds, it was over. Sophie saw with relief that the chestnut foal with the white socks stood next to her mother, waving her tail as if unaware she had ever been in danger.

"You did good," Shane panted, riding to Sophie's side.

"It was Cisco." Sophie slumped forward, gasping, to stroke his mane. "I knew I could trust him."

✳ ✳ ✳ ✳ ✳

Hours later, Liv was stuffing cold canteens into saddlebags to go look for Bando. Diego's herd was safe in the Lucky Star corral, enjoying fresh hay and water. None of the mares or foals had suffered from the stampede and long trek back to the ranch. The small chestnut filly stood close to her mother, enjoying a meal of warm milk.

"Tell me again," Liv said to Sophie, her eyes wide. "Did the mares really stampede? Weren't you scared? I wish I'd been there!"

"There wasn't time to be scared." Sophie took a canteen from her hand. "Cisco was amazing ..." She stopped looking up. "Who's that?"

Liv turned to see Dayna and Cheyenne ride up to the corral on Silver Spur palominos.

Dayna threw herself off Champagne and strode toward Shane. "I was so sorry to hear about Navajo," she cried. "How is he?"

"A bit lame and stiff is all," Shane said, pulling his hat down low over his eyes. "What are you two doin' here?"

Making trouble, Liv thought furiously. There was no time to deal with Dayna and Cheyenne now. Bando, that poor baby, was out there in the desert all alone. Shane had saddled Trixie, the bay with the white markings and they were all set to leave – their mom had volunteered to come along to help.

"We came to see you," Cheyenne was speaking only to Shane. "I want you to come back to town with me. I'm sure you'd be more comfortable with your own family. Can't these here twins look after Navajo?"

Shane shook his head. "Can't discuss it right now," he muttered. "Have to look for a lost colt out in Wild Horse Creek canyon."

"Oh! Is that why you're all saddled up? We could help," Cheyenne said. "Couldn't we, Dayna? We're very experienced ridin' in this country."

For a second, Dayna looked unsure of what to say. Then she tossed back her pigtails. "I guess we could. For an hour or two. I'd have to be home before dark."

But we don't want you, Liv wanted to shriek. She knew Dayna didn't care about the little colt. She was just volunteering to look for Bando to please Cheyenne.

74

"Come along if you want to." Shane shrugged. "The more help we have the better."

"If you two girls are going, I'll stay." Jess Winchester handed her saddlebag of supplies to Dayna. "I'd like to be close to the phone in case Pop calls with news about Mom's operation. But please, all of you get back before dark."

"Don't worry about us, Mom," Sophie said. "The horses and Tux can see in the dark and we've got lights."

Liv was still fuming. "Call Temo on your cell," she suggested to Dayna. "Maybe he can come and help too."

"Temo's working." Dayna glared down her nose at Liv. "He's got no time to be ridin' around lookin' for stray colts."

Liv wanted to say something really rude but they had to get moving. They needed to find Bando today. With the herd back on the ranch he was helpless on his own.

CHAPTER 9
The Search Begins

The sun was slanting low over the mountains, turning the desert floor dusky pink as they took the trail to Wild Horse Creek Canyon. Their horses threw long shadows as they loped along the sand road to the canyon's mouth.

As the red rock walls of the canyon closed in on either side they had to ride single file. Dayna took the lead with Shane and Cheyenne behind him, then Liv and Sophie. Tux bounded beside his master.

"Come on, Cisco," Sophie whispered. "I know you're tired but let's try to keep up."

The sorrel horse did his best, but by the time they caught up, Shane and Dayna, Cheyenne and Liz were sitting silently on their horses gazing down at the bodies of Carmelita and the lion in Coyote Canyon.

I don't want to look, Sophie thought. *I'm going to keep*

*on remembering Carmelita the way she was – chasing
after her colt – beautiful and free.*

"Which way do you think Bando would run?" Liv was
asking Shane.

"Not sure." Shane squinted up at the canyon walls.
"This side's too steep." The east wall of the canyon was a
sheer cliff. There was no way a colt could have climbed it.

Shane pointed to the other side of the canyon. "And
on that side there's nuthin' but boulders and ledges and a
few dry caves ..."

"Ugh!" Dayna interrupted with a shiver. "I hate
caves. Spooky, dark places. You won't get me in one
of those."

"It's more likely Bando hightailed it along the canyon
bottom," Shane went on. "We'll look here first. Might be
better if we split into two groups."

"Who elected you trail boss?" Dayna asked, her hands
on her hips.

Shane frowned. "It's my fault the horses got left out
here when they never should have," he growled, "when
Diego wasn't ready to defend his herd. My fault his colt
is lost. You can do whatever you want, but my idea is that
you and Liv ride up the west side of the canyon. Sophie
and Cheyenne and I will take this side."

"All right." Dayna shrugged. "You don't have to get
all huffy. I was just askin'."

"Take Tux with you," Shane looked down at his dog.
"He's a better tracker than I am."

"All right." Liv grinned. "That way there's three of us on each side. C'mon, Tux. Good boy, come with me."

Tux whined, with his head on one side, looking up at his master.

"Go on, Tux," Shane ordered. "Go with Liv and Dayna. Find the colt."

As if he understood every word, Tux gave one sharp bark as if to say, "Let's go!"

Sophie felt a stab of annoyance. Why couldn't Cheyenne go with Liv and Dayna? Shane and I don't need her, she thought. But at least she was with Shane and not searching the other side of the canyon.

Dayna and Liv were soon out of sight, hidden by clumps of trees and brush.

"Look under every mesquite bush and live oak," Shane warned Sophie and Cheyenne. "Bando could be hunkered down low to the earth, hidin'."

Hiding or dead, Sophie thought. Nobody said it, but she knew the colt's chances of survival were few. A coyote could have got him, or another cougar, or a bald eagle swooping down from the cliffs above. The important thing was to find him – before something else did.

Letting Shane and Cheyenne ride close to the canyon wall, Sophie rode Cisco along the cracked mud of a dry wash. She remembered how, just a few weeks ago, a flash flood had swept through these canyons. The raging water tore trees from their roots and tumbled boulders as if they were pebbles.

All that water had drained away almost as quickly as it had come. Except for the Lucky Star spring, this whole vast land was dry.

You'd never know it had rained, Sophie thought, except for the wildflowers that had bloomed a few days after the storm. She knew she was lucky to see them. Many of these plants only flowered after a big flood. But even though she loved the desert flowers and liked Shane – a lot – she'd never feel at home here. Not like Liv who'd loved the desert from her first sight of it.

Sophie brought Cisco to a sharp halt. Was that something in the shadow of an overhanging rock? A cool, sheltered place where a colt might hide from the sun. Sophie leaned down from Cisco's side to look.

It was only a desert fox, stretched out in the shade, sleeping. Sophie could see its large ears and one long paw draped over the smooth rock.

"Anything?" Shane called.

"Just a fox," Sophie answered. At the sound of her voice the fox opened its eyes and shot out from under the overhanging rock. It disappeared in the brush.

Sophie straightened in the saddle and rode on. The end of the canyon was still an hour of tough riding away. She wished she could feel at home in the desert, like that fox.

CHAPTER 10
Where's Tux?

Liv and Dayna rode along the far bank of the canyon without talking. *Dayna looks like she was born on horseback*, Liv thought enviously. There was no effort to sit straight, no tension in her neck and head. Her broad straw hat protected her from the sun and the leather chaps she wore over her jeans kept the thorns from prickling her legs.

She isn't even trying to find Bando, Liv realized, as she untangled her own jeans from the thorns of a wait-a-minute bush. *We should be searching every gully and under every low-hanging tree for him.*

Liv was about to yell at her to slow down when she heard Tux barking from the wall of rock above her right shoulder. She scanned the steep slope with her eyes but there was no black-and-white dog. Patches of green oak and brown bunch grass were the only signs of life. The canyon wall was a jumble of huge boulders, some leaning against each other, some standing alone. At the top of the canyon wall five jagged rocks thrust up like a fist raised at the blue desert sky.

"Dayna, wait," she called ahead. "I hear Tux up there." She pointed at the tumbled rocks.

She saw Dayna slowly turn Champagne and head back at a slow walk.

"Why would Shane's dog go up there?" she drawled.

"Maybe he found Bando." Liv tried to keep the sarcasm out of her voice. "Isn't that what we're all trying to do?"

"I don't hear any barking," Dayna said doubtfully.

Liv blew out an exasperated breath. "Well, I heard him. Are you coming with me to look, or not?"

"Oh all right, but this is a total waste of time," she heard Dayna mutter behind her. "We're never gonna find that colt alive."

"Don't be so sure." Liv called over her shoulder as she leaned forward to help Cactus Jack climb over the stony surface. "These Spanish horses have survival skills your fancy palominos could only wish for."

Dayna caught up. "That's a laugh." She shrugged. "My dad says your grandparents' horses are just scruffy little leftovers from the past. The herd is down to, what? Thirty-three horses now and it's gonna keep shrinking. So much for their survival skills."

"We can build it up again. And there are thirty-*four* horses if we can find Bando."

Now it was Dayna's turn to be sarcastic. "And how do

you plan to build it up? I thought you were leaving in a couple of months."

Liv answered without thinking. "We might not leave. We might stay and help Gran and Granddad."

"Oh, really?" Dayna scoffed. "Even if you did stay, how are you two greenhorns gonna be able to save this herd?"

Liv didn't answer. She realized she'd made a mistake sharing her dreams with Dayna. Dayna might not be as vicious as her father, but she had no love for the Lucky Star ranch or its horses. The two ranches had been rivals for the land and the precious water in Wild Horse Creek Canyon for generations. Bad news for her grandparents' herd was good news for the Silver Spur Guest Ranch. And as their horses scrabbled up the rocks, Liv knew Dayna was probably right. She and Sophie were too young to really make a difference.

"Tux is not up here," Dayna puffed a few minutes later. "There's no sign of him."

"I heard a dog," Liv insisted. "He might be in there." She pointed to a dark cavity under a huge boulder wedged between two other stones.

"You're not going under that hangin' rock!" Dayna protested. "It could come crashing down on your head."

"It's been there for a long time." Liv squinted up at the boulder. "What makes you think it'll collapse now?" She turned to Dayna, her eyes flashing. "Go back down if you want to, but I'm surprised a desert expert like you would wimp out so fast."

"You'd better watch what you say." Dayna frowned. "We tolerate a lot of crazy talk from tourists around here, but we start to get fussy when people stick around like they own the place."

"I have just as much right to be on this land as you do." Liv glared at her. "My family settled here more than a hundred years ago."

"But your mother married a northener and went away." Dayna raised her eyebrows.

So that settles it, Liv thought. *As far as Dayna's concerned, Sophie and I will always be outsiders. Because of something our parents did. It's not fair.* "I'm going in anyway," she said.

She stripped off Cactus Jack's bridle and hung it on a branch of the oak. She tied Jack's lead rope to another. "You'll be nice and cool here," she told him, stroking his sweaty neck. She took the survival pack from the saddlebag and slung it around her shoulder.

"Why are you taking all that stuff?" Dayna demanded to know.

"Not sure what I'll find in that hole." Liv shrugged. "It's better to be ready for anything." She threw a challenge over her shoulder. "Come with me, if you dare. If not, tell Shane and the others where I've gone."

Dayna flushed red. She got off Champagne and tied her beside Cactus Jack. "I'll come, but this is stupid," she muttered. "There's likely not enough room for a jackrabbit's ears under there – no space for a dog, let alone a colt."

CHAPTER 11
The Hanging Rock

Dayna was wrong. As she and Liv stooped under the hanging rock, they found a hollow space big enough for both of them to stand.

"E-ew!" Dayna clapped her hand to her nose. "It stinks in here."

"Might be an animal's den," Liv murmured, turning her light on a heap of dried leaves and twigs.

Dayna nodded, still holding her nose. "Tux coulda chased the animal out. But there's no sign of that dog, so let's make tracks." She turned to go.

"Wait." Liv grabbed her arm. "Look, Dayna – this isn't the end." The narrow beam of her light showed a slit in the cave wall to their right. Beyond was darkness.

"If you think I'm goin' in there –"

Dayna's protest was interrupted by a distant yelp.

"That's Tux, for sure," Liv cried. "Maybe he's found Bando."

"And maybe he's found another cougar." Dayna twisted out of Liv's grip and ducked for the cave entrance. "He's just a dumb dog."

"Shane's dog," Liv reminded her.

"All right, Shane's dumb dog! You are really startin' to get on my nerves, you know that?" Dayna muttered.

Liv shone her light on the gap. "Looks like a tunnel – wide enough for Bando to get through. I'm going in. You do whatever you want."

Dayna squirmed back through the entrance. "I'm gonna get my own light, that's what," she shouted over her shoulder. "You wait for me, you hear?"

Liv waited impatiently while Dayna got the light from her saddlebag and joined her.

They slipped through the slit in the wall.

The gap widened to a downward sloping passage. Liv went first. Their lights bounced off gleaming walls and pillars of stone. Their feet crunched on fine gravel. In some places the cave seemed to come to a dead end, only to open up again around a corner into a high, domed room. In other places, the passage became a ledge along a yawning dark hole.

"This cave is enormous," Liv gasped after five minutes of twists and turns.

"I'm not ... going on," Dayna said in a quavering voice. "This is far enough for me."

"What's wrong?" Liv turned to shine her light on Dayna. The girl's face was glossy with sweat even though the cave was cool.

"I hate caves," Dayna panted. "What if our lights went out? It would be pitch dark in here. And where's Tux? We can't even hear him now."

"You go back then." Liv turned her light back to the cave floor. She recognized real fear in Dayna's face. She looked like Sophie when she was scared of being in a high place.

"Fine, I will." Dayna spun on her heels and headed back toward the cave entrance. Liv saw the light dim as the beam from Dayna's flashlight bobbed away. Liv stood and listened to her footsteps fading. When they had died completely, she moved on. "Tux!" she called. "Where are you, boy?"

✳ ✳ ✳ ✳ ✳

Sophie, Shane and Cheyenne had reached the end of Coyote Canyon where the ground sloped up to a gravel ridge. There was no sign Bando had come this way. Not even Shane, trained in tracking, could find one small hoofprint or mound of miniature manure.

"Might as well go back," he grunted.

Cheyenne jockeyed for position closest to him. "Mebbe Dayna and Liv found him," she said. "They had Tux to help."

Sophie watched in frustration as they pulled ahead, chatting to one another.

"You let that fancy palomino mare nudge you out of the way," she scolded Cisco in a whisper.

Cisco snorted as if to remind her there was such a thing as horse etiquette and he was just being polite.

"You stay here in the center, Sophie," Shane called to her. "Cheyenne and I will ride back along the other side."

"That does it," Sophie sighed, giving up. Shane was never going to think of her as anything but a friend, a little sister at best. He forgot all about her when Cheyenne was around.

She almost wished a big rattlesnake or mountain lion would appear. In the past, Shane had rushed to her rescue when she was threatened by wild animals.

But the day was too hot for snakes. Cisco's head went down and his lip drooped as he walked. Sophie struggled to keep herself upright in the saddle. Glancing over, she could see Shane and Cheyenne weren't having any problem staying awake. In fact they seemed to having an argument. Shane had rammed his hat down with one hand and Cheyenne pounded her saddle horn as she made a point.

What could they be fighting about? Was Cheyenne still trying to talk him into coming to live in town with her family?

She saw Shane turn and ride back toward her. *Good*, Sophie thought. *He's had enough of Cheyenne's pestering*. "Don't worry," she said as he settled Trixie in beside her. "We'll find Bando."

Shane's face cleared. He shoved back his hat so his fine hair showed. "You sounded like your grandmother right then," he said with a grin.

"I wish Gran would come home," Sophie gulped.

"When she's around, everything feels right." *Shane must be feeling a huge weight on his shoulders*, she thought. *Granddad left Diego's herd in his hands and now Carmelita is dead and her foal is lost. Plus he has his own father to worry about.*

Cheyenne clattered back to them on Flash Dance. "Shouldn't we have met up with Dayna and Liv by now?" she asked Shane. "We're halfway down the canyon."

"I was thinkin' the same thing," said Shane, tipping his hat down. "I'm sorta surprised I haven't heard Tux barkin', too." He clucked to Trixie, and she picked up the pace along the east side of the canyon.

Sophie was close behind when Shane held up his hand to call a halt. "I see tracks." He pointed to the ground, then up the canyon wall. "Headin' up there."

"Up to those rocks?" Sophie said nervously. She didn't like high places.

Shane and Cheyenne had already started the climb. Sophie struggled to keep up with the better riders, leaning forward to help Cisco.

Minutes later they found Champagne and Cactus Jack tied to the trees. Sophie jumped from Cisco's back to check them. "The saddlebags are empty. Where are Liv and Dayna?"

Shane bent lower and studied the sand in front of them. "More tracks here. Looks like paw prints, small hooves and a couple of footprints."

"Tux and Bando!" Sophie pointed to the triangle-shaped

cavity under the hanging rock. "They must have gone under that boulder. And Dayna and Liv went after them."

"Why don't we wait out here for them?" Cheyenne asked. She was still in the saddle. "The sun will soon be going down and Dayna has to be home before dark. Her dad gets awful mad if she keeps the horses out too late."

CHAPTER 12
Fear

Bando was frightened. He had run as fast as his young legs could carry him from the terrible sights and sounds of his mother's death. Instinct had pushed him to find a place to hide.

He had found a refuge under the hanging rock. The family of marmots who lived there had moved out at his approach.

Then the dog had come. As far as Bando was concerned, Tux was a predator like the coyote – an animal that glared at him with fierce eyes and had a mouthful of sharp teeth. All he knew was to run as far and as fast as he could.

Tux had driven him deep into the cave and cornered the colt in a domed cavern. There a narrow shelf overhung a deep pit. Tux barked fiercely at Bando, trying to herd the colt away from the danger.

Bando's fighting instinct kicked in. He might be cornered, but he wasn't giving up without a fight. In fury, he wheeled and struck out with his small hoofs.

Tux wasn't ready for the attack. Before he could dodge out of the way a glancing blow from Bando's hoof sent him flying over the edge of the ledge, down into the pit below. He landed with a thud, and lay as if dead on the sandy floor in the darkness.

Bando fled along a side tunnel.

✳ ✳ ✳ ✳ ✳

Dayna wished she hadn't acted so impulsively. She hadn't realized it would be so hard to find her way back to the entrance under the hanging rock. The path had seemed clear enough when they entered. Now it twisted and turned like a corkscrew.

"Just keep going up," she told herself. "The entrance is at the top." But even up and down were not clear. The path dipped and rose, twined around rock pillars and bent back on itself.

"I've been here before," Dayna whispered. She recognized a smooth fall of rock. It glistened red when her light fell across it. She'd been going in circles.

Should she shout for Liv? No, that would be too embarrassing. She fought down the fear that threatened to sweep over her. "Keep left," she said out loud. "No right turns." That way she'd either find her way out or meet up with Liv again.

Many twists and turns later, Dayna found herself forced to climb. The cave wall ahead was steep. It fell away to a narrow crevice on the right. Needing both hands to climb, she gripped her flashlight between her teeth, planted one foot in a crack in the smooth rock face and hauled herself up. She could see where the tunnel continued at the top of the incline. If she could just reach it she could keep to her plan to go left.

As she climbed, Dayna felt a rush of wind on her face, heard the flapping of wings in the air. Bats! she opened her mouth to scream. The flashlight dropped from her mouth, clattering away down the slope. "No!" she screamed. Her hand shot out to grab it. In her dive for the light she lost her balance. Before she could stop herself she was falling, falling, slipping through the darkness, the sound of her own scream echoing in her ears.

Seconds later, the crevice walls closed around her, slowing her free fall. Her right foot found a firm place to stand. Her flashlight was gone.

Heart pounding, her breath ragged, Dayna scrabbled for a foothold with her left foot. There! She was standing with one foot on either side of a steep dark fissure into which she fallen. She felt around the space with her hands. It was as narrow and smooth as the inside of a chimney. Nothing to hold or grip.

"HELP!" Dayna screamed. "Somebody, help me!" It was as though she was at the bottom of a well. The

darkness was total. Her footholds were all that kept
her from falling deeper into the crevice where she'd be
wedged between the rocks – unable to breathe or move
in any direction. She could hear bat wings flapping at the
top of the crevice. Waves of panic engulfed her.

CHAPTER 13
Tracks in the Sand

Liv was far from the spot where she and Dayna had separated, descending to the deepest part of the cave. The air was stale and hot. Liv found herself stopping often to catch her breath. "Not enough oxygen down here," she panted to herself. "I hope I find that 'danged dog,' as Shane and Dayna call him, soon."

She went on calling for Tux. Some parts of the path were steep and she had to sit and slide down. It was at the bottom of one of those slides that she landed on something pointed and hard.

"Ow!" Liv shouted, her cry echoing around the high hollow chamber. "What's that?"

She rose to her knees. She'd landed on the corner of a metal can, almost buried in coarse sand.

Liv scrabbled with her hands at the sand so she could read the label on the box's top, then sat back on her heels. Kerosene. The label was clear. It showed an old-fashioned lantern full of oil. Someone had been exploring this cave with kerosene lamps. That must have been a long time ago – before flashlights and batteries.

Moving carefully, she explored the rest of the chamber. Something red caught her eye – a scarlet smudge on a round rock. It looked as though red powder had been ground in the hollow of the rock. This was much older than the lamp oil, Liv was sure. People must have been coming down here for ages. The question was – was anyone here now?

Liv shone her light around the low-roofed cavity. It angled off to the right. She squeezed under an arch of stone and found herself on a ledge looking over a chamber as deep as a two-story room.

What was that on the floor? Something black and white, but it wasn't moving. "Tux?" Liv gasped.

The dog lifted his head and let out a groan.

"Oh, Tux!" Liv cried. "Hold on, I'll get you out." Circling the ledge, looking for a way to climb down, she found a long pole leaning against the chamber wall. It had crooked boards nailed across it as rungs. People had been here, all right, and they must have used this pole to reach the bottom of the chamber.

But how old was the makeshift ladder and would it hold her weight? Liv stuck her flashlight in her jeans' pocket, beam up. She needed both hands to climb.

The rungs wobbled as Liv started down. She half slid

down the pole, holding it with both hands, all the way to the bottom. She landed ankle-deep in sand.

Liv plunged through the sand to Tux's body. "Poor boy," she soothed and was rewarded by Tux opening one eye and licking the hand she held out to him.

"How did you manage to fall off that ledge?" Liv spoke gently, patting his head. "Were you chasing Bando – was that it?" It was a long fall, and Tux might have died if he had not landed in such deep sand. "I wish you could talk, buddy," she crooned, "so you could tell me where it hurts and how this happened to you."

Liv shone her light around the chamber, looking for another way out. But the chamber was like a sink, with smooth, high walls and no exit.

It was decision time. Should she leave him here, try to climb up the pole ladder and find help? She couldn't carry him up the pole, even if it was wise to move him.

Tux gave another moan. Liv smoothed his coarse border collie hair with her hand and felt the dog relax under her touch. "I'm not going to leave you," she promised. "We'll wait here together for someone to come. At least for awhile."

✳ ✳ ✳ ✳ ✳

"I'm not going in there!" Cheyenne repeated, tipping up her stubborn chin. "Might be something gross in a cave like that. Dangerous animals, or bats."

"Stay here if you want to," Shane said gruffly. "I'm going to follow these tracks in the sand as far as I can.

They lead into this gap." He unbuckled his saddlebag, found his flashlight and shone the light into the dark space under the hanging rock.

"I'm coming with you." Sophie quickly tied Cisco beside Cactus Jack.

Cheyenne made a face. "You're leaving me here all alone?"

"Take care of the horses," Shane told her. "If we're not back at sunset, ride back to the Lucky Star ranch and get help."

Cheyenne glowered at Sophie. "Oh, all right. But this is dumb. How do you know that hole leads anywhere?"

"Because the tracks go in, but they don't come out," Shane said. He shoved his hat down tight and stooped to squeeze into the low entrance. "Come on, Sophie."

As they headed into the dark tunnel leading to the larger cave, Sophie glanced back at the sunlight streaming under the hanging boulder.

"Wait a minute, Shane," she said, grabbing the sleeve of his plaid shirt. "Lend me your knife." She knew Shane kept a folding knife in his pocket.

"What do you want this for?" Shane dug it out and handed it to her.

Sophie snapped open the largest blade. "I'm going to scratch the wall here so we can find our way back," she said. "I know you're a brilliant tracker, but just in case."

She could see Shane's grin in the flashlight beam. "That's pretty smart, for a greenhorn."

Shouting and calling for Tux, they wound their way through the cave's tunnels. At every fork and turning Shane paused to study the faint tracks in the sand. "Looks like the colt, and Tux, and at least one pair of boots," he told Sophie.

"What is this place?" Sophie asked as she carved another arrow in the wall. "Could it be a cougar's den?" At every turn in the tunnel she'd been afraid they'd meet a pair of glowing cat's eyes.

"No animals down here. There's no water for 'em to drink." Shane straightened up and his head brushed the ceiling. "Some of these dry caves go underground for a long way. Years ago the Apache people used to store food in 'em, and there's a legend that a gang of outlaws used to hole up in a dry cave somewhere near Rattlesnake Bend. Maybe this is the one."

"Outlaws?" Sophie gasped. One more thing in this desert to worry about.

"Long time ago," Shane said. They went on, calling for Tux.

It wasn't Tux that finally answered. Instead, as they started down another tunnel they heard a faint cry from far below.

"That's Liv!" Sophie cried. "LIV!" she bellowed. "Where are you?"

Following the sound of her voice, she and Shane soon reached the brink of the high domed chamber. They looked down and saw Liv with Tux's head cradled on her lap.

"Now how in the name of jumpin' jackrabbits did you two get down there?" Shane called softly.

Tux looked up and whined with joy at the sound of his master's voice.

"Tux fell. He's hurt." Liv gestured with her chin. "I climbed down that old pole ladder."

Sophie could hear the concern in her sister's voice. "Don't worry, Liv," she called, "we'll get you out of there."

"I don't know if it's safe to move Tux," Liv faltered. "What if his back –?"

"Is he movin' his head and legs?" Shane asked.

"He tries to raise his head," Liv called back. "But he hasn't gotten up yet."

"Feel his back and legs like you would a horse," Shane called. "Just gently. See if you can tell where he's hurtin."

They could see Liv pressing her fingers along Tux's spine. When her hand slid down his back leg, he let out a yelp.

"Might have broken his leg, maybe his hip," Shane said in a worried voice. "I'd better come down there and help you get him up. The thing is –" He investigated the ladder. "I don't know if this'll hold my weight. It could have been here since the outlaw days – seventy, eighty years or more." He shrugged. "Guess I'll have to give it try." He turned to put his boot on the first fragile crosspiece.

"Wait." Sophie had been thinking. "Take off your shirt."

CHAPTER 14
Shane's Shirt

"Did you just tell me to take my shirt off?" Shane stared at her. "Why on earth would I do that?"

"For T-Tux," Sophie stammered in her eagerness to explain. "Throw your shirt down to Liv. She can use it as a sling to carry Tux up the ladder. She's lighter than you are."

"Like one of those baby slings," Liv called from below. "Brilliant. Do it, Shane."

"All right. But I hope you girls know what you're doin'."

Shane stripped off his shirt, weighted it with a small stone and threw it down to Liv. He and Sophie watched as she gently worked the cloth under Tux's body, then lifted him and tied the sleeves around her neck. His head hung out one side of the sling and his tail out the other.

"If that ain't the darndest!" Shane exclaimed. "It might work."

Sophie knelt at the edge of the ledge and tried to steady the pole as Liv climbed the crooked rungs, focusing her own energy like a beam to give Liv strength.

Liv carefully tested each wobbly crosspiece with her foot before putting her weight on it. One of them cracked and fell away, but she had already reached for the next and pulled herself up with her arms. Sophie and Shane reached to help her up the last long step. At that moment the pole snapped in two and fell to the bottom of the chamber behind her.

"Phew!" Liv gasped. "I don't think I'd like to try that again!

Shane untied the sleeves from around Liv's neck and scooped Tux into his arms, shirt and all. He felt carefully around the dog's hind end, with Tux madly licking his face and whining with joy the whole time. "I'm pretty sure nuthin's broke," Shane said. "Just mebbe twisted, or sprained."

He smiled. "Tux looks pretty good wearin' my shirt, don't you think?"

Sophie hugged Liv hard. Tux looked good in anything at this point, and Shane looked amazing without a shirt. She was glad he couldn't see her blushing in the dim light.

"That pole ladder was really old. Who do you think left it here?" Liv asked.

"Shane says there was a gang of outlaws that used this cave," Sophie told her.

"Bank robbers," Shane added. "They were pretty famous around here."

"I found a can of lamp oil," Liv said, "but it looked really ancient."

"Things stay well-preserved in caves like this." Shane looked around the domed chamber. "There's lots of small openings to let in air, and of course there's no water. Used to be wet, though – thousands of years ago. That's how all those pillars got formed."

Shane, still carrying Tux, walked carefully along the ledge, searching the path with his light. "Looks like he was following the colt when he fell," he said. "Bando's tracks keep going this way."

"We've got to find him," Sophie said. "He must be so scared and hungry and lost." She looked around the domed chamber. Someone else was missing. "Where's Dayna, Liv?"

"Didn't you see her when you came in?" Liv looked surprised. "She hated the cave, so she headed back for the entrance."

"We didn't see her." Shane and Sophie shook their heads.

"Maybe she rode home." Liv looked at her watch. "It's getting late."

"No," Sophie said slowly. "Champagne was still tied up beside Cactus Jack. She wouldn't have gone home on foot, would she?"

"No way," Shane said.

"Then she must still be somewhere in the cave," Liv

said slowly. "The place is humungous. I hope she isn't lost." She reached for Tux. "Let me carry him, Shane, so you can focus on tracking Dayna."

Shane nodded and gently handed Tux over. Liv cradled Tux in her arms, while Shane and Sophie searched each side tunnel for tracks made by the sharp-toed cowboy boots that Dayna wore. The border collie was heavy, but he seemed to like staying close to her, Liv thought. She would carry him as long as she could.

"Do you think Dayna could have come this far?" Sophie panted after many long minutes of walking, sliding, and climbing.

"Easy to get confused and panic." Shane scratched his head. "But it's funny we don't hear her hollerin'. Sound travels good down here."

Minutes later, Sophie held up her hand. "Stop! I *do* hear something."

They paused. The echoes of their footsteps on the gravel faded. Other sounds, faint scrapings, came from a passage just ahead.

As they turned the corner, flashlights gleamed on a pair of glowing eyes.

"Woof!" Tux gave a sudden startled bark.

The eyes disappeared in a blink, replaced by the thudding of small hoofs fleeing away from them down the passage.

"It's Bandera!" Liv shouted. "Come back, we won't hurt you."

But Bando was already far down the tunnel, running as fast as his weakening body could carry him, spurred on by terror.

"Tux, you danged dog," Shane scolded. "Why did you have to go and bark like that?"

"We'll never catch up to him now," Sophie grieved.

Tux squirmed in Liv's arms as if he knew he'd done something wrong. "He was just acting like a dog," Liv stroked his head. "And Bando was acting like a foal who's been raised on the range and doesn't know dogs or people."

"We could follow his trail," Sophie said eagerly. She shone her flashlight on the small hoofprints left in the sand.

"Hold on a minute, look!" Shane bent low. "Those look like Dayna's boots, scuffed over by the colt."

"She must have gone down this tunnel," Sophie said. "Let's go."

But Liv, still hugging Tux, felt a sick dread. Why wasn't Dayna calling for them?

I should have stopped her from heading back on her own, Liv thought. *If she's lost, it's my fault.*

✳ ✳ ✳ ✳ ✳

At the Silver Spur Ranch, Dayna's father Sam strode back and forth on the barn floor beating one fist into the palm of his other hand. "I don't like the thought of my horses bein' out there after dark, let alone my daughter. Too many cougars around." He stopped to peer at the fading light coming through the large barn doors.

"Where in tarnation did Dayna and Cheyenne ride off to?" he shouted at Temo.

Temo came out of a stall with an empty feed bucket. "I think they rode over to the Lucky Star ranch, *Señor*." He spoke politely to the older man.

Sam Regis grew red in the face. "How many times have I told Dayna I don't want her hangin' around Ted Starr's spread," he yelled. "And I especially don't want my purebred mares anyplace near that worthless Spanish stallion of his."

"*Si, Señor*,' Temo agreed, but this time there was a smile on his handsome face that Sam couldn't see in the darkening barn. The idea of calling Diego worthless was a joke to Temo. There never was a finer horse; a true throwback to the brave stallions brought by the Spanish explorers and bred for years to withstand the worst the desert could throw at them. In Temo's opinion, Diego was worth a hundred of Señor Regis's horses.

"You're finished with your shift," Sam went on. "Ride over and fetch my daughter for me, will you?"

Temo nodded. "With pleasure, Señor." He didn't mention that he'd worked twelve hours and hadn't had his dinner yet. He headed for the tack room to pick up his saddle. His black-and-white paint Helado was munching his evening portion of hay out in the Silver Spur corral.

"And tell her to get her disobedient little butt and my horses back here before I get good and mad." Sam stalked out of the barn.

CHAPTER 15
Temo's Secret

"They went to Coyote Canyon to look for the colt," Jess Winchester told Temo. "He must have run off when his mother was killed by the cougar."

"Poor Carmelita," Temo murmured.

The two of them were in the Lucky Star ranch yard, Temo on his horse, Jess shivering as the desert night chilled with the setting of the sun.

"They should be back," Jess told him. "They left hours ago. Dayna said she had to be home before dark."

"That's why I'm here." Temo nodded. "Her father is very angry."

"I'm not exactly pleased myself," sighed Jess. "I can't go and look for them because I'm waiting for a call from my father about my mother's operation."

"I understand," said Temo. "I'll go. If Señor Regis phones, please tell him where I've gone."

"If Sam Regis calls before Pop does, I probably won't answer," Jess said briskly. "I want to keep the line free. But after I talk to Pop I'll give the old buzzard a call."

"*Gracias.*" Temo gave a polite bow of his head, wheeled Helado around and rode out of the ranch yard.

As the desert darkened and the stars came out, Temo rode along the sand trail to the canyon, knowing his horse could see the way clearly. He stopped at the spring to let Helado drink and heard the high lonely yip-yip-yip of coyotes coming from the smaller canyon ahead. "The song dogs," Temo said to himself. "Coyotes on the hunt."

Careful not to ride near a ledge or outstretched branch where a cougar could be waiting to drop on Helado's neck, he rode into Coyote Canyon. So this was where Carmelita lost her life. He took off his large black hat and bowed his head to honor the brave mare who had given her life for her foal. She had been a wonderful lead mare, a fitting mate for Diego, a mother to his finest foals. She would be a great loss, he thought.

"So where is your baby, brave Carmelita?" he asked sadly. "Maybe already with you in the heaven for horses." Temo knew Liv, Sophie and Shane would not give up searching until they found the colt or his body. What was more puzzling was why Dayna and Cheyenne were still out here looking. It didn't fit their characters, he thought. Not at all.

He was not surprised to hear hoof beats and see Cheyenne riding toward him in the dusk on Flash Dance.

"Temo! I'm so glad to see *somebody*,' she cried. "I waited as long as I could outside that stupid cave."

"*Lento*. Slow down." Temo caught Flash Dance's bridle. "What cave? Where are Dayna and the others?"

"Up there," Cheyenne pointed. "Where the canyon gets narrow. Come on, I'll show you."

Temo urged Helado after Cheyenne's horse. How had Cheyenne and Dayna become separated? Had something happened to Señor Regis's daughter? He jammed his big black hat down tightly on his head to keep the worried thoughts from buzzing in his brain. Not Dayna! Nothing must happen to her!

❄ ❄ ❄ ❄ ❄

Bando trotted on in the darkness. Small and surefooted, his hoofs found the level path, his whiskers told him when he was near a rock wall, even when the cave was so black he could barely see. His nose told him that somewhere ahead was fresher air.

Behind was the dog who looked so much like the coyote that had attacked him. Like all horses, the colt would never forget a bad experience. Those snapping jaws and pointed ears were imprinted on his young brain. He would not turn around and go back.

He had been many hours now without his mother's precious milk. Bando was tired, hungry and above all puzzled. Where had she gone?

Another colt might have given up the search, but generations of survival instinct led Bando forward.

Somewhere there was food and warmth and the comfort of his kind. He must just keep going until he found them.

At some spots in the cave, fissures in the rocks let in the moonlight and air. Here Bando stopped and tried to find a way out, a way back to his mother and the herd, but the passages were too small and too high for him to escape.

❄ ❄ ❄ ❄ ❄

Dayna was pinned in one of those fissures. She could turn her head, but her shoulders and hips were almost imprisoned in the narrow rock chimney.

For a while she had been barely conscious from shock and terror. Even if she had heard voices calling her name she would not have had the strength to answer. Now, as consciousness returned she remembered her foot slipping, remembered struggling to keep her other precarious foothold, then losing her balance and slipping deeper into the crevice – scrabbling desperately at the wall in a attempt at getting a grip with her fingernails.

I've totally destroyed my manicure she thought, giggling to herself hysterically. *Oh help, I'm so unbelievably thirsty!*

The worst of it was she could hear water, trickling somewhere far below her. If she could only reach it! It was maddening. How could you forget how thirsty you were when the sound of running water was so clear?

Where was everybody? How dare they leave her stuck here like this? She was Dayna Regis. She wasn't the kind of girl who fell down holes in caves and died of thirst. *Somebody help me!* she raised her head to roar. But her throat was too parched and her chest squeezed too tight to let out anything but a hoarse whisper. The painful sound echoed horribly in the narrow chimney.

❆ ❆ ❆ ❆ ❆

Tux heard. He growled and squirmed in Liv's arms.

"What's the matter, boy?" Liv lowered him gently to the ground and untangled him from Shane's shirt. Tux took a forward hop, holding his injured leg close to his body.

Shane reached for his shirt. "I'll take that, if Tux is finished with it."

"It looks like he hears something – maybe it's Bando come back," said Sophie as Shane handed her his flashlight and struggled into his shirt. The narrow tunnel was barely big enough for him to shove his arms into the sleeves.

At that moment they all heard the unmistakable sound of jangling spurs behind them. "Who's there?" Sophie cried out.

The sound came closer. Liv's flashlight gleamed on Temo's wide-brimmed hat. "*Hola amigos.*"

Liv felt her heart thump – she was so glad to see him. "Temo! How did you find us?"

"Some clever person has been scratching arrows on the rock." Temo grinned. "Who was that?"

"Sophie," Liv said. "She thought it would help us find our way out of here."

"Sophie, you are very smart." Temo bowed his head. "Cheyenne showed me the entrance and we have been following your marks." He shrugged. "It made it easy to find you."

At that moment Cheyenne wriggled under Temo's arm and thrust herself in front of his sturdy frame. "Where's Dayna?" she demanded to know.

"We're lookin' for her," Shane explained. "She left Liv and went to find her own way out, but she must have got lost and –"

"Dayna's *lost*?" Cheyenne's voice rose to a shriek. "You've *lost* her?"

Meanwhile Tux had continued hopping down the dark passage, his nose to the ground, his ears pricked straight up. Now he sat awkwardly and let out another yelp.

"Hold on, Chey," Shane said. "Tux is tryin' to talk. Maybe he can lead us to Dayna." He scooped up his dog. "Hey there, buddy, you're too hurt to walk. Let me carry you."

But Tux wiggled so strenuously Shane was forced to put him down. Nose to the tunnel floor, hopping on three legs he led them forward. When he reached a steep slippery rock face, he stopped, sat and whined.

"What's the matter now?" Cheyenne raised her voice. "Oh, ugh! Bats!" They flitted around the tunnel, sometimes in the flashlights' beams, other times flapping near their faces.

"Hush! Listen," Shane said. "The bats won't hurt you."

Silence fell in the cave. Now they all heard a muffled cry for help.

"Up there." Temo started up the smooth slope ahead. He shone his light into the crevice to the right. "Dayna!"

Liv saw the look on his face, reflected in his flashlight beam. It was shock, and something else. Terror for Dayna. *He cares about her*, Liv thought, *a lot more than he ever lets on!*

"Get me out of here!" Dayna's voice sounded hollow and far away.

"*Si, muchacha.* Don't worry. We'll get you out." Temo turned to them with a frightened look in his dark eyes. "She is wedged in a tight crack," he gasped. "No room to get a rope around her."

Liv took a deep breath. "Sophie, give me a boost so I can get up there and shine another light."

"Yes, come – *venir*!" Temo whispered urgently. "Help me, Liv."

CHAPTER 16
Out of the Dark

Sophie saw the pain in Liv's face as she prepared to join Temo. She knew what her twin was feeling exactly as if her own heart was hurting. It was so clear that Temo wanted Liv – but only to help Dayna. Up to now, Temo had hidden his feelings for Dayna under a laughing, distant mask. But now, when she was faced with real danger, his emotions were as clear as the beads of sweat on his forehead.

She gave Liv a boost and her sister started up, her boots scrabbling on the smooth surface. Sophie watched her find a perch from which to shine a light into the crevice while Temo leaned forward, softly calling.

"Dayna. Speak to me, *por favor*. Can you turn your body so your back is against the wall?"

There was no answer. Just a long pause. Sophie held her breath.

"Liv, shine your light this way," Temo ordered, grasping Liv's wrist to turn the flashlight.

"*Bueno*. Good," he murmured. "Now, Dayna, brace both feet against the other wall. *Mucho bueno*."

Another long pause, then, "Don't cry, my Dayna. You can do this. Now, move your back up a little, then your feet. *Un poco*, a little, now a little more. I know it is hard, but you can do it. Soon the passage will get wider. Your arms will be free and you can use them to help you. *Un poco, un poce mas*. Just a little more."

Sophie could see the sweat trickling down Temo's forehead. He was fighting every bit of the way with Dayna. She watched him reach down to pull her up to him. Saw Liv's anguished glance as Dayna melted into Temo's arms, her face hidden on his shoulder.

Then they pulled apart, as if remembering who they were and that people were watching. Dayna straightened her pigtails where they had come loose from their elastics. Her face was streaked with dirt and tears but the proud, haughty look was back in place. Temo's own face had closed down as if a curtain had been pulled across it.

Then he smiled his familiar, teasing grin. "We should give you a badge for rock climbing," he said. "That was very good."

"I don't need a badge. Just give me something to drink." Dayna slid down to the others with Temo and Liv behind her. "I was dying of thirst the whole time I was

down there and it didn't help that I could hear running water right under my feet."

Temo said in a shaky voice, "There is water in our canteens, back at the entrance. Let's go. *Vamanos*."

Cheyenne rushed to hug Dayna. "I was so scared for you!"

"I'm fine," Dayna said, but Sophie noticed that she was leaning heavily on Cheyenne as they headed back along the tunnel.

"Are you sure you heard water, Dayna?" Shane called ahead to her. "This here's a dry cave – has been for thousands of years."

"Well, maybe it has been dry, but it's not now." Dayna turned to peer at him. "I'm telling you, there's water down at the bottom of that hole I was stuck in. It sounded wonderful – cool, fresh – oh! I'm so thirsty."

"This is important, isn't it, Shane?" Sophie whispered. "It could be a new water source for the Lucky Star ranch."

"If they could pump it to the surface," Shane murmured. "It would mean your grandparents' tanks would be full. They could raise cattle again..." He paused and went on in a lower voice. "I wonder if Dayna's going to tell her dad. The water source might even be on Silver Spur land. No tellin' how far we've traveled underground."

"What about Bando?" Sophie gave Shane's sleeve a tug. "Are we just going to forget about him?"

Shane put an arm around her shoulders. "I'll come back and search the cave tomorrow," he promised. "But now we should head for the ranch. Your mother will be worryin'."

Sophie knew that was true. Besides, they were all exhausted and Tux needed to get checked by a vet to make sure his leg wasn't broken. But she also knew that the chances of finding Bando alive the next morning were slim to none.

✳ ✳ ✳ ✳ ✳

Sam Regis was waiting with a horse trailer at the Lucky Star ranch. Jess stood back, arms folded, while he ordered everyone around.

"Load up my horses. I don't want them out on the trail after dark," he started to bluster, and then saw Dayna's face and dirty clothes. "What happened to you?" he growled. "No, never mind that now. Get in the truck, girl. Temo, get Champagne and Flash Dance in the trailer."

Liv saw Temo give Dayna a piercing look from his dark eyes as he turned to obey. She looked like a person who had just been struck by lightning. They had been standing close together and as they moved apart their feelings were so strong you could almost see the bond burning between them.

Liv felt her heart lurch. Dayna would never dare let her father know how she felt about Temo.

"Are you coming back to town with us, Shane?"

Cheyenne asked as she slid into the truck's cab beside Dayna.

Shane was holding Tux close to his heart.

"After all," Cheyenne went on. "These here aren't relations to you."

"You aren't Shane's relation either." Sophie flung the words at Cheyenne. "Just because your stepmother's his aunt doesn't make you his cousin."

"Quit that!" Shane glared at Sophie in disappointment. "I think I'll hitch a ride with you back to my trailer," he said to Cheyenne. "I should check in with my dad and stay there tonight."

Liv gave Sophie's arm a squeeze in the darkness. Mom had been right. Shane couldn't stand girls fighting over him. He was going back to that awful trailer.

"I'll be back in the morning," Shane was telling their mother, Jess. "Once I get the vet to look after Tux, here."

"Don't worry," Jess told him. "I'm sure the girls will look after your horse. Thank you, Shane, for helping get them home."

"I didn't do much," Shane said slowly. "Liv and Sophie looked after themselves real well out there. If it wasn't for Liv, I might not have Tux, here. And if it wasn't for Sophie, none of us might have found our way out of that cave." But he didn't look at Sophie or smile at her, Liv noticed.

"I'm proud of both my girls." Jess smiled.

When the Silver Spur truck had rolled away, Jess gave

a deep sigh. "Poor Dayna," she said. Liv glanced at her, startled. Had her mother noticed how Dayna felt about Temo, too?

"That father of hers has a one-track mind," Jess went on. "Do you know he offered to buy this ranch a few minutes ago? Didn't even wait to see if Dayna was all right. All that man thinks about is getting Pop's land and his spring."

"We'd better get Cisco, Trixie and Cactus Jack untacked and fed," Liv said. Her mother hadn't noticed. She'd been too busy being annoyed with Sam Regis.

"We'll be in in a minute, Mom," Sophie added. She stopped suddenly, remembering. "Was there any news about Gran?"

"Good news." Their mother's face brightened in the light from the house. "She came through the surgery well." She paused. "Don't stay out here too long. You must be exhausted and starving."

Liv and Sophie led the horses across the ranch yard. They didn't talk. Both their hearts were too full.

In the dimly lit barn, the two of them worked slowly, taking off saddles and bridles, brushing the three horses' sweaty backs, making sure there was water and hay in the corral.

"What a mess I made of things," Sophie sighed at last, smoothing the brush down Cisco's side. "I practically threw Shane into Cheyenne's arms. Why did I have to go and embarrass him in front of everybody?"

120

"At least Shane isn't hopelessly in love with someone else." Liv stared straight ahead, the currycomb motionless in her hand. "Did you see the way he looked at her?"

Sophie knew Liv was talking about Temo. "I saw."

Liv leaned against Cactus Jack's warm chestnut shoulder for comfort. "It's so hopeless. Temo would never look at me like that in a million years," she said sadly. "And Dayna's not good enough for him."

"I know," said Sophie, straightening Cisco's mane, "but I feel sort of sorry for her, too. She's been hiding her feelings for Temo, maybe even from herself. Out there, in the cave, when he was helping her, there wasn't any place to hide. She's in trouble. I don't think her father would let his daughter date a lowly cowhand."

"I know!" was Liv's anguished cry. "But I don't care! She's rich and can have everything she wants. Why should she have Temo, too?"

The two of them walked their horses out into the desert night. The stars were a bright blanket covering the dome of sky above the ranch. The moon had set over the mountains. Liv opened the corral gate and they slipped the halters off Trixie, Cisco and Cactus Jack and let them go to find their scattered hay.

Navajo, Shane's horse, came over to whicker at the other horses. He thrust his nose in Liv's pocket as if to say, "I'm lonesome. Where's Shane and his evening treat for me?"

"Navajo's walking a little easier than this morning," Liv said.

"Was it just this morning?" Sophie couldn't believe it. This felt like the longest day of her life. In less than twenty-four hours they'd found Carmelita's body and that of the mountain lion and lost Bando. She'd helped start and then stop a stampede of horses, with Cisco's help. She'd helped rescue Tux and Liv and Dayna and witnessed Dayna and Temo falling in love. At the end of it all she'd embarrassed Shane and maybe lost his friendship.

She stroked Navajo's smooth hide. "He's almost Helado's twin," she murmured. "Except Helado's black and white instead of brown and white. I wonder what the English word is for *helado*."

"Ice cream," Liv said with a catch in her voice. "Temo told me Helado reminds him of his favorite flavors – chocolate and vanilla."

"Horses are so much easier to understand than humans," sighed Sophie, stroking Navajo's soft nose.

❋ ❋ ❋ ❋ ❋

Bando could smell water. He had been traveling upwards through the winding cave passages for some time, heading for fresher air. Now this watery smell put new energy in his tired young legs.

The foal had recently learned to drink water. He preferred his mother's milk, but now he was starved and thirsty and he headed for the rank odor. Under one of the cracks to the surface, a pool of rainwater had gathered in a shallow depression in the cave floor. Most of it had evaporated and what was left wouldn't have interested a horse used to clean water. But desert horses like Bando had survived because they took advantage of every drop of moisture they could find.

Bando clattered up to the edge of the rock bowl and slurped water eagerly. Then he shook his head as if to get rid of the strange taste and went on. The cave was lighter. He was near another opening – this one on the other side of the canyon wall. It was large enough for Bando to slip through.

When he trotted out into the open air he was high on a hillside. Stars twinkled overhead and the air was sweet and cool. Bando raised his nose, curled back his lip and took a long sniff. Horses! There were horses somewhere down below. Perhaps that's where he'd find his mother. All of his instincts called him down the hill and toward that wonderful smell. But his body was too tired to go on and he sank down behind a mesquite bush, stretched out on his side and slept.

CHAPTER 17
Helper at Dawn

Sophie prowled the ranch house living room, too tired to sleep. She picked up the picture of her grandfather, Ted Starr, mounted on Diego, galloping across the desert. Granddad in his white hat, white shirt and silver belt, riding the blue roan stallion.

Tears pricked her eyes. Bando would never grow up to look just like Diego after all. The stallion was older now, like her grandparents. He might not be fathering many more foals like Bando! It felt as though everything was coming to an end. Sophie picked up another photo of both her grandparents – young, smiling, one on either side of a dark bay horse with a white blaze down his nose. He reminded her a bit of the mysterious stallion that had appeared to challenge Diego, only the stallion was black. Sophie supposed they both had Spanish colonial blood flowing through their veins.

Liv appeared from the kitchen, a cheese sandwich in her hand. "Want one?" she asked.

"I can't eat." Sophie plopped down on the leather couch and pulled the striped serape over her. "I keep thinking of Bando down in that cave, and Gran in the hospital, and Shane –" She gulped. "Shane's in that trailer with his dad."

Liv put her sandwich down. "Now I don't feel like eating, either." She looked at Sophie, her usually sunny face a mask of despair. "What are we going to do, Sophie? How are we going to tell Gran and Granddad that Carmelita, their best mare, is dead and Bando, her last foal, is gone too? How can Gran get better when she hears news like that? It will break her heart."

✳ ✳ ✳ ✳ ✳

As the taillights of the Silver Spur truck and horse trailer turned slowly around, Shane walked up to his lonely trailer on its patch of desert scrub with Tux under his arm.

The door was locked. He banged on it but there was no answer. "Dad!" Shane called. "Are you lockin' me out? We need to talk."

There was still no answer. The trailer was dark. With a feeling of dread, Shane walked to the old pickup, still carrying Tux. He opened the cab door, fished under the front seat for the spare key and found it, sticky with truck dirt.

Wiping it on his jeans, Shane walked back to the trailer door. "Dad! I'm comin' in."

The trailer was dark inside and smelled of fried meat and beer.

Shane got a towel from the tiny bathroom, bunched it up on the floor with his foot and lowered Tux onto it. "Stay there," he said.

It didn't take long to search the trailer. Nobody was in either small bedroom. With a sigh of relief, Shane sank down at the small central table.

Then he saw the note, scrawled in shaky handwriting. "*Dear Shane,*" it read. "*I'm real sorry I lost my temper. I hope Navajo and you can forgive me. I'm takin' a taxi to Rattlesnake Bend. I'm going to the clinic and I hope they send me to rehab right away. If I'm not here when you get back that's where I'll be. Take good care of yourself. Harlan Tripp, Your dad.*"

Rehab! Shane read the note again. His father had tried rehabilitation before. Maybe this time it would work.

He fed Tux some dog food and found a can of tuna and some crackers for himself. "Too late for the vet," he told Tux. "This'll hold us till we get some of that good breakfast grub tomorrow at the Lucky Star."

✳ ✳ ✳ ✳ ✳

As the sky over the mountains to the east turned pink the sweet smells of the desert dawn prickled Bando's nose. He lifted his head, shook it and let it flop again, closing his eyes. His mother was nowhere to be seen.

But there was a smell of horse. Bando opened his eyes once more and struggled to get his long colt's legs under him. Finally he was on his feet. And there, calmly grazing bunch grass was a mountain of a horse. A black horse. A stallion who turned to look at him.

Bando knew how to behave. He made chewing motions with his jaws, letting the stallion know that he was not a threat. Just a harmless baby.

The black horse blew and went back to grazing bunch grass.

Bando got up and tried to take a few nibbles. He had four teeth, two of them fairly new, and none of them much used to eating grass. He whinnied to let the stallion know he was hungry.

The stallion could have told Bando that he wasn't the only hungry animal on that hillside. A family of coyotes had been circling Bando when he arrived and he had driven them away. A cougar had screamed from a high ledge sometime during the night. Now it was dawn and time for the stallion to move on. He took a few paces away, without looking back.

Sure enough, Bando followed. They made their way down the hillside away from the cave, the black horse stopping often to let Bando catch up. The colt was weak and would have lain down again except that the stallion had a magic string that seemed to pull him forward and give him strength.

It was all downhill until they reached a level plain. In the distance were the roofs of ranch buildings, red in the rising sun.

The stallion wouldn't go much closer. He had been

chased by men from that ranch. The men had ropes
and rifles. They had pursued him in a giant bird with a
whirling blade. The stallion had been chased before by
helicopters. He had seen his wild brothers trapped in
chutes made of ropes, driven by the rattling bird in the
sky. He had no desire to run into that kind of trap.

He stood on the edge of the ranch lands where there
was an open gate, waiting for Bando to catch up. Then he
whinnied and nudged the colt through the opening. From
here, they could see a herd of mares and geldings in a
large corral.

The black stallion gave another whinny, wheeled and
galloped away.

Bando started after him, and then realized he couldn't
keep up. On wobbly legs he went back to the gate,
through it and on toward the corral.

CHAPTER 18
Bando Belongs

It was early the next morning when the phone rang at the Lucky Star ranch.

"Liv!" her mother called from the ranch house door. "Phone for you. It's Dayna Regis."

Dayna! Liv thought with a jolt. *I don't want to talk to her.* She shut the corral gate and walked to the house, taking her time, trying to stop the churning in her stomach. *She's going to say something about Temo and I'm going to lose it – I just know it.*

Dayna's voice was breathless when Liv finally picked up the phone. "What took you so long? You've got to get over here right away. Your colt's here."

"Bando?" Liv shouted. "Are you sure?"

"Of course I'm sure. The colt we spent all day looking for. He's here."

Liv gasped, "Sophie and Shane just left for the

cave. I'll try to catch them. We'll be there as fast as we can."

She stared at the phone in her hand. Back home in Vancouver a quick call would have reached Sophie, but Sophie didn't have her phone with her, and even if she had it probably wouldn't work in the depths of Coyote Canyon.

"Mom!" she yelled. "Fill a couple of canteens for me while I saddle Cactus Jack. I have to go find Sophie and Shane. Dayna thinks she's got Bando."

"At the Silver Spur?" Jess came hurrying from the kitchen, a dishtowel in her hand. "It sounded from what you said that Bando was lost in the cave. How would he get way over to the Regis ranch?"

"I have absolutely no idea." Liv was already racing out the door. "And Dayna may be wrong."

Minutes later, her mother stuffed two canteens of water in her saddlebags as she headed out on Cactus Jack. "Be careful!"

Liv knew this was no time to be careful. Dayna had said to hurry.

✳ ✳ ✳ ✳ ✳

Sophie and Shane had left Tux behind, sleeping on an old saddle blanket in the box on Shane's truck.

Shane had arrived at dawn, hungry and silent. "Vet's not open till one o'clock," he'd said to Sophie. "We might as well go look for Bando this morning."

They'd saddled and bridled Trixie and Cisco in silence

and rode out of the Lucky Star without a word. Sophie could see Shane was upset, and it was more than losing Bando. "I'm sorry I said what I did when Cheyenne – wanted you to go with her," she mumbled as they rode toward Coyote Canyon. "It wasn't my business."

"Oh, Cheyenne." Shane's thin face twisted into a scowl. "She's always after me to be some kind of family to her, or boyfriend, I don't know what." He turned in his saddle to look at Sophie. "If I was lookin' for a girlfriend, which I'm not, but if I was ... well, never mind."

Sophie gulped. What had Shane been going to say? That he wouldn't choose Cheyenne, that maybe he'd choose *her* if she were older?

Shane went on, "But if it was family I wanted, it wouldn't be my aunt's. It would be your grandparents, and your mom and Liv and you."

"It would?" Sophie felt a huge weight lifted from her shoulders. The sun seemed to sparkle on the dry dusty desert as they rode along. Shane hadn't said anything about his own father, but this wasn't the time to ask. "That's okay with me." She tried to sound casual. "I – we can be your good friends – like family."

"That's fine." Shane gave her a shy grin then bent to study the sand at his side. "Keep your eye out for Bando in case the little fella found his way out of the cave. He'd most likely head back here where he last saw his mom. He'll be lookin' for other horses and he'll smell Cactus Jack and Trixie."

"And maybe without Tux barking at him he won't be

so scared," Sophie said. Minutes later they heard hooves clattering over the dry stones and turned eagerly to look. But it wasn't Bando; it was Liv, riding recklessly up the canyon trail.

"Wait!" she waved her arms and shouted when she caught sight of them. "Wait for me!"

Half an hour later the three of them rode into the Silver Spur ranch yard looking for Bando.

"Over there." Liv pointed. They could hear loud neighing coming from an area behind the big Silver Spur barn. They quickly dismounted, tied the three horses to the hitching rail and ran for the corral where they could see Temo's dark head and Dayna's fair one, bending over something on the ground.

It was Bando, lying just outside the fence.

Inside the fence was a palomino mare, neck outstretched, sniffing at the foal from between the bars of the pole fence.

They could hear Temo and Dayna arguing as they approached. "I don't know what you are waiting for," Temo shouted. "Golden Girl lost her foal last night. Bando needs a mother."

"My father –" Dayna began.

"Forget about your father."

"But you could get fired."

Yesterday, Liv thought, *Dayna wouldn't have let on that she even cared if Temo got fired. Today it's enough to make her go pale under her tan.*

As they raced to help, Liv saw Temo and Dayna lift the limp body of the foal. Bando tried to struggle. If his mother or Diego had been there they would have let the colt know the young man and the girl were trying to help him, but Bando was a range colt and people were new and strange. He lashed out with his sharp little hoofs and thrashed in Temo's and Dayna's arms. They were face to face – Dayna pale with strain, Temo's dark eyes fierce with love.

Liv couldn't stand to see the looks on their faces. She ran and threw open the corral gate. Shane and Sophie hurried to help Temo and Dayna carry Bando through. The other horses all clustered around as they laid him on the ground, but Golden Girl showed no special interest in him.

Sophie knelt beside Bando. She stroked his neck and rubbed his floppy legs. "Stay with us," she whispered. "We're trying to help."

"Did you find him ... like this?" Liv choked.

Dayna shook her head. "He was standing when we first saw him. Just outside the corral like he was looking for a way in. He must have been there most of the night."

"Where is the body of the foal Golden Girl lost?" Temo asked Dayna suddenly.

"Still in the foaling box." Dayna's face turned paler. "My father wanted the vet to examine it."

"Help me find a rag. We will rub it over the dead foal and then over Bando," Temo said. "Sometimes that helps the mare accept the orphan."

Dayna gave a quick nod and led the way toward the barn.

"Will that work?" Sophie looked up at Shane.

"It might." Shane bent down to feel the pulse in Bando's throat. "A mare often won't accept a foal this big, but if it smells like her own, she might."

"Will Bando be strong enough to nurse?" Liv asked.

"Hard to say. But this little fella has a lot of fight in him. I wonder how in the world he got here." Shane looked up at the hills that rimmed the canyons. "It's a long piece away from the cave."

"We could take him home. We could bottlefeed him," Sophie suggested.

Shane shook his head. "It would take too long to get him to trust us," he said. "If Temo's plan works it will be faster and better."

Temo and Dayna were running from the barn carrying an old blanket. Behind them bustled a very red-faced Sam Regis.

"I don't know what in thunderation you think you're doin'!" he stormed.

"Just stay out of the way, Daddy," Dayna told him. "I'll explain later."

"But that ... that's ..." spluttered Sam at the sight of Bando's body. "That's one of Ted Starr's foals." He swiveled on the heels of his cowboy boots and directed his anger at Liv and Sophie. "If you two girls think for one dashed minute I'm havin' one of Diego's colts in my corral –!"

"It isn't their idea, Daddy," Dayna said firmly. "It's all mine." She gave Temo a half-embarrassed glance. "Temo! Do what I tell you. Rub that blanket all over the colt and then bring Golden Girl over where she can get a good sniff at him."

"*Si, Senorita* Dayna," murmured Temo in his old meek manner, but Liv could see the glint of laughter in his eyes.

Moments later Golden Girl was nosing Bando as if he was a new foal, and he was struggling to his feet. Another moment and he was guzzling down her life-giving milk and soon his flag of a tail had started to wave again.

"I won't stand for this," Sam Regis roared at Dayna. "What makes you think I will tolerate my prize mare feeding Ted Starr's worthless colt?"

"Señor," Temo started to protest.

"Never mind, Temo," Dayna broke in. "Daddy, listen to me. You'll tolerate it because it makes good horse sense. And because yesterday, these girls and Shane saved my life – with a *little* help from Temo." She shrugged her proud shoulders, "And because having this colt in your corral will be good ammunition the next time you fight with Ted Starr over water."

This last argument made Sam Regis frown, then nod. "All right, daughter," he said gruffly. "Let him stay, till he's weaned."

Liv and Sophie shared a look. It was easy to predict what their grandfather would say if he saw Diego's foal

in Sam Regis's corral. "I hope Bando is weaned by the time Granddad gets home," Liv whispered to Sophie."

"Did you tell your father about the water in the cave?" Shane was saying to Dayna as they all watched Sam Regis stalk away from the corral.

Dayna shook back her two blonde pigtails. "Nope. I'm keepin' that piece of news to myself right now. You never know when it might come in handy." She looked after her retreating father with a smile.

"Anyway, thanks to you," Sophie said, "I think Bando's going to be all right."

"I guess I didn't do it just for Bando." Dayna said honestly. "I was afraid Temo and my father were going to get in a fight. They ... they don't see eye to eye about certain things, like Spanish barb horses. I didn't want Daddy ordering him off the ranch, or something like that." Her voice trailed away.

"Anyway, thanks," Liv fiddled with Cactus Jack's mane so Dayna couldn't see her face. "That means a lot to us, to our grandparents."

"You're welcome." Dayna shrugged, then smiled. "I know. Come back to see him tomorrow. We'll have a dip in the spa pool, and a massage and lunch. We can use it after that horrible cave and bats in our hair."

"They don't really get in your hair, you know," Liv said quietly. "Bats have echolocation. They never hit anything."

"Well, it feels like they're in your hair," Dayna

shivered. "And you, Shane Tripp, you're not invited to the spa, but come for lunch, anyway. We'll have a picnic and you boys can barbecue."

"Great plan!" Sophie said.

Liv narrowed her eyes at Dayna but didn't say anything. If Temo was cooking and they were eating outside, Dayna wouldn't have to banish him to the kitchen. Was that her real plan?

CHAPTER 19
Liv Decides

"I think Navajo will be fine to ride tomorrow," said Shane later that day, as he watched his paint horse amble up the pasture toward the fence. "He's movin' well now."

"That's good," Sophie climbed the fence and sat on the top bar. "You never said how your dad was last night."

"He wasn't home." Shane tipped his hat down. "Checked himself into rehab up in Tucson. So I guess I'll have the trailer all to myself for awhile."

"You don't have to stay there," Sophie blurted. "You're welcome to sleep in the bunk house."

"I know, but I shouldn't leave our place empty." Shane reached through the bars to pat Navajo. "I should be there in case Dad comes back. He's never made it through a whole rehab before. Things have been tough for him since my mom left." He rubbed Navajo's cheek. "But who knows? Mebbe this time he'll try harder."

"I hope so." Sophie longed to throw her arms around Shane, to comfort him in his trouble. Her own family problems seemed so small compared to his. She blushed to remember her romantic dreams of being swept into Shane's arms. Now she'd be happy just to be his friend, at least for a long time to come.

Shane gave Navajo a final pat. "Anyhow, this fella's eaten enough of your hay. He's got plenty of his own back at the trailer."

Sophie knew this was Shane's way of saying he wanted to leave. It was no use trying to persuade him to stay. She swallowed hard and changed the subject. "Can you come to Dayna's barbecue tomorrow?"

"Don't see why not," Shane nodded. "I'll take Tux to the vet first and then drive over." He grinned. "We have to keep an eye on Bando, after all."

The next morning, Sophie woke up to find Liv stomping around the bedroom.

"I don't want to go to the stupid spa." Liv pitched one of her riding boots at the wall.

"Liv!" Sophie sat up and stared at her. "What's wrong?"

"I can't stand to see the way Temo and Dayna look at each other. It's like ... it's like ..."

"Romeo and Juliet?" Sophie finished with a sleepy yawn. "Can you imagine what Dayna's father would say if he knew how Dayna felt? Or her stuck-up mother? Or Temo's family, for that matter? They need their jobs at the Silver Spur Ranch."

"I have feelings, too." Liv raged.

"I know, but you're going to get over it. We're too young to be serious about guys, or so Mom and everybody tells us. Dayna and Temo are seventeen and eighteen. This could be once in a lifetime love."

"Is that supposed to make me feel better?" Liv hurled her other boot at the wall.

"No, but just think about it." Sophie got up off the bed and started for the door. "It's time for breakfast and then we have to feed and groom the horses." She went out shaking her head.

Her mother met her at the foot of the stairs. "What time will you be heading out for the Silver Spur?" she asked with a smile. "I'm glad you're making friends around here. I knew it would just take time."

"Talk to Liv!" Sophie pointed up the stairs. "She doesn't want to go."

"I'll talk to her," Jess promised. "And when you both get back from Dayna's I want to discuss taking a quick trip to Tucson to visit Gran in the hospital and get Pop moved to a better motel."

✳ ✳ ✳ ✳ ✳

At ten-thirty Sophie saddled and bridled both Cactus Jack and Cisco, hoping Liv would change her mind. As she slipped Cisco's bridle over his ears and straightened his noseband she sighed. "Why does Liv get so crazy sometimes? she whispered. "It's like she's the only one in the world who has feelings." Cisco blew softly in

reply and looked down his lovely nose at her as if he understood every word she said.

Outside the barn Sophie met Shane and Navajo, ready for the ride to the Silver Spur. Tux had been seen by the vet, had his back leg bandaged and was resting once more in the back of Shane's truck.

He and Sophie leaned on the corral fence, watching Diego in the corral with his mares.

"How's he doing?" Sophie asked.

"He's itchin' to get out of this corral and back up the canyon, I can tell you that," Shane laughed. It was true, Sophie thought. Diego looked like a regal pillar of strength and energy this morning. He prowled the fence as if measuring it for a jump, his glossy gray blue hide only slightly showing the scars from his battle with the black stallion.

"But we'll wait for your Granddad to give the word." Shane took off his hat and put it back on again. "He's the boss."

"Do you think Diego will know his son when we bring Bando back?" Sophie asked.

"Sure he will. He'll probably have to teach him some manners once Bando's done hangin' out with that spoiled overfed bunch at the Silver Spur, though."

"Spoiled like their owners," Liv added as she arrived at the corral with water canteens for all of them.

Sophie handed her Cactus Jack's reins. "Glad you're coming," she whispered.

Shane hopped up on Navajo. "Dayna might be spoiled, but I have a lot more respect for her after the way she stood up to her Dad," he mused. "Not sure why she did it, but it took guts."

"She had her reasons," Liv muttered. "Let's go."

Sophie felt nervous as she swung her leg over Cisco's back and followed Liv down the road to the ranch gate. Her twin sister was as cheerful as a thundercloud. Would this lunch at the Silver Spur be a disaster?

CHAPTER 20
Showdown at the Silver Spur

"Temo's been barbecuing all morning," Dayna sighed happily.

Sophie didn't feel reassured watching her and Liv in the spa pool. Dayna was obviously in a world of her own. She lay back against the swirling jets of water, her face glowing and the faraway look in her eye softer than before.

Liv hovered near Dayna, looking glum.

Cheyenne and Hailey didn't seem to notice anything. They chatted away about Hailey's healing shoulder and Cheyenne's terrifying experience with bats in the cave.

By the time they'd had their massage, dressed and dried their hair, Dayna looked perfect. She was wearing a pale pink dress that set off her tan and matching sandals. It was obvious she'd planned this barbecue to impress

Temo. She'd already mentioned his name sixteen times –
Sophie had counted.

"Temo's meat for the *birra* is going to be so-o good,"
Dayna sang out as she led the way to the outdoor
courtyard.

"What's *birra*?" Liv asked.

"It's Temo's special recipe," Dayna sighed. "From his
mother, Marita. Isn't that a lovely name?"

"But what is it?"

Dayna twirled the end of one pigtail around her finger.
"It's a kind of delicious Mexican stew, and Temo will cut
off slabs of the meat he's been cooking to put in it, and
you'll just die it's so good."

Nineteen times, Sophie thought.

They drifted into the courtyard where barbecue smoke
and spices perfumed the air. The picnic table was set with
colorful ceramic plates and bowls, and in the middle was
a big platter of chopped onions, cucumber, tomatoes,
cilantro and radishes. A colorful *pinata* in the shape of a
horse hung from a beam over the table.

Sophie had seen Mexican *pinatas* at birthday parties
back home in Vancouver. They were covered in colorful
tissue paper and full of inexpensive little gifts. Kids
whacked them with sticks until they broke and the
presents showered down. As they tramped in, Temo
turned from the big stone barbecue with a long grilling
fork in his hand. He froze at the sight of Dayna. Once
more, it was as though the two of them were alone in the

sunny *ramada* with its roof of woven grass and the light filtering through on their faces. No one else mattered.

A short woman with her hair piled high on her head hurried from behind the barbecue with a platter of tacos in her hand. "Temo, aren't you going to introduce me to your new friends?" she asked with a smile. "Temo, what is wrong? Are you sick?"

"*No, Madre*," Temo muttered, but he still couldn't take his eyes off Dayna.

Dayna's mother, Brenda Regis, picked that exact moment to stride in from the spa. "Howdy, everybody," she crooned. "Hope you're all hungry as coyotes." She glanced at her daughter, who was still gazing at Temo with lovesick eyes.

"Dayna, what's the matter with you, honey?" She looked Dayna up and down, then her eyes went to Temo, and then to Temo's mother. The two women stiffened.

Say something, Sophie prayed silently to Dayna. *Order Temo around in that bossy voice of yours. Quick, before your mother and his mother figure this out.*

But Dayna stood stunned, incapable of speech.

Sophie gave Liv a nudge. "Follow my lead," she whispered and then in a louder voice shouted, "Hey, is this a good time to break the *pinata*?" She dived forward to snatch the long fork from Temo's hand. "Whee!" she shouted. "Fun! Come on, everybody. Let's see what's inside!"

She poked at the paper horse. Liv grabbed a barbecue

brush and bashed at it too. Cheyenne and Hailey joined in with shouts of glee. The paper horse flew to pieces, scattering small objects and cactus candy all over the picnic table. Some fell into the punch bowl with a splash. More landed in the salad plate. Laughter and confusion broke the spell of tension in the air as they all dived for the *pinata's* prizes.

Dayna snapped out of her trance. "Look what I've got!" She held up a plastic whistle, then blew a shrill note. "Time to eat, everybody."

Temo turned back to the barbecue. The spell was broken, the danger past. His mother, Marita, gave him another frightened glance, but went on laying food on the table.

Dayna's mother picked a piece of candy out of her hair and said, "Well! We usually break the *pinata* after the meal, but I suppose it doesn't really matter."

They all sat down and dived into lunch. The Mexican food was delicious. Stuffed with Temo's delicious *birra*, tacos, enchiladas, flautas and flan and cactus candy, the seven flocked to the corral to see Bando and his adopted mom, Golden Girl.

"They look like they've always been together," Sophie sighed. "I hope you'll let us come and work with Bando in the next few weeks. I want him to know who we are."

"Sure." Dayna was studying her with a surprised expression. "That stunt you pulled ... breaking the pinata when my mother came in ... you did that on purpose, didn't you?"

"I had to do something." Sophie grinned. "You and Temo looked, well, you know."

"It was because Dayna looked so *hermosa*, so beautiful," Temo said softly. "For a minute I couldn't catch my breath."

"And you looked so –" Dayna didn't finish. Her eyes had gone dreamy again.

"Hey!" Hailey cried. "Are you guys in love or something?"

Dayna and Temo exchanged embarrassed glances.

"You are!" Cheyenne gasped.

"We have to keep it a secret from everybody," Dayna said firmly. "You too, Chey, if you want to stay my friend."

"As if I'd tell," Cheyenne crossed her heart.

"Shane, are you in, *amigo*?" Temo asked.

"I don't even know what you're talkin' about." Shane shrugged. "But I never talk to anybody about my friends."

"Good, then it is a pact." Temo said.

They leaned on the corral fence and watched the band of lovely golden horses with their one blue roan colt.

Dayna reached for Sophie's and Liv's hands. "You two passed the first test," she said. "You're part of the group – part of us." She gave a wicked grin. "Next test, school on Monday."

Liv chuckled. "School's going to be easy. Making friends – that's hard."

She smiled and Sophie knew that her twin sister was going to recover from her broken heart. Liv would be her usual take-charge self by the time they walked through the school door in Rattlesnake Bend, Sophie predicted happily.

Meanwhile, they had a trip to Tucson to see Gran and Granddad to look forward to. After that, there was lots of work to do with Bándo, and riding Cisco every day after school. Just thinking of those rides made Sophie's heart glow with happiness. It was amazing how she'd come to love that red-gold horse in just a few weeks – how much he felt like part of her.

Sophie looked over to where Shane was laughing with the others at Bando's antics. It was okay to be just Shane's friend, she decided. More than okay. She gazed up at the rim of distant mountains against the desert sky. *Who knows*, she thought, *I might even start to feel at home here. If there is a new source of water the Lucky Star ranch won't be so dry and dusty anymore – I could plant a garden!* It was going to be a fantastic summer.

Afterword

Liv and Sophie's grandmother, Sandra Starr, lay back in her hospital bed. Sophie sat on one side of the bed, Liv on the other.

"A few weeks on the ranch has made all the difference." Gran smiled at them. "Now you really look like my granddaughters."

"You look good, too, Gran," Sophie said. It was true. Their grandmother looked much better than one would expect after an operation. There was color in her cheeks and her smile was as wide as ever.

"Tell me all the news from the Lucky Star," she begged. "Oh, how I've hated being away. I can't wait to get home."

Sophie and Liv glanced at each other. The moment had come when they had to tell Gran about Carmelita.

She listened as Sophie told the story of finding the mare's body.

"My beautiful friend," Gran cried when she had finished. "How I will miss her. She was one of the best horses our ranch ever raised. I trained her as a little filly and she was so good, so easy to train." She paused. "What happened to her foal – the little roan colt?"

"He got away." Liv said, squeezing her grandmother's hand. "We call him Bando right now, short for Bandera, and he's wonderful."

"But you can rename him when you get home," Sophie quickly added.

"No," Their grandmother shook her head, her blue eyes bright. "I think Bandera is a perfect name. We will keep it. Tell me again – what happened to the cougar?"

"Carmelita killed it," Sophie said.

Their grandmother sighed. "Then Carmelita lived as she should and died as a good brave horse might," she said. "She gave her own life to save the life of her foal. And that's how she will be remembered."

Gran lifted each of their hands and kissed them. "You will tell her story to your own granddaughters some day," she told them. "As long as there are horses like Carmelita and people to tell their stories the life of our ranch will go on."

Sophie and Liv shared a look. Without speaking, the twins had the same thought. Maybe this was a good time to tell Gran about the water in the cave. Water would bring more life to the ranch just as their grandmother was getting well.

"Gran," Sophie said, "We have something else to tell you."

"And this is good news." Liv gave her grandmother a big hug.